An Orphan's Goodbyes: A Memoir

JAMES BROWN

Published by JAMES BROWN, 2023.

AN ORPHAN'S GOODBYES: A MEMOIR

First edition. December 18, 2023.

ISBN: 979-8227514363

Written by JAMES BROWN.

Table of Contents

This book is dedicated to the three people whom I live for—first, my wife, Charlotte, my guardian angel sent to help me with her duties to guide me to the place where I was supposed to become a contributor to the human race. Her love for me comes directly from God. It is that special.

Second and third are my sons, Jimmy and Greg. They are an inspiration and a comfort to my soul, a companion to my heart, and a contribution to the human race.

An Orphan's Goodbye

A Memoir

James Brown

Chapter 1

Georgia Brown

At the depot in Kansas City, a train's whistle gave two short blasts—a final warning to passengers that the train was ready to depart. A young woman tightly holding a swaddled baby in her arms quickened her pace as she approached car number 28. Her long, hurried strides and her gloved hand waving at the conductor were accompanied by her desperate-sounding voice, as she called out, "Wait! Please!"

As the conductor helped her step up on the little stool that he had placed on the platform for those boarding the sleeper car, her large, flowered, canvas bag slipped off her shoulder and almost landed on the ground. The conductor caught it just in time.

"It's okay, ma'am. I've got it," he said in a reassuring tone.

He took her canvas bag and followed her into the passenger car as she slid into an empty seat. He placed her flowered bag in the seat next to the window. Then he tipped his hat at her and returned to his location to pick up the small stool.

She nodded and smiled as she straightened her navy-blue-and-white-striped cardigan over her skirt. She let out a long sigh and was grateful that baby Jimmy had slept through the whole ordeal. She placed him gently on her lap and proceeded to remove her yellow-brimmed hat and the stick pins that held it in place to her dark brown hair. Carefully opening her bag, she removed a little plastic case and tucked the stick pins inside.

Suddenly there was a big puff of steam billowing up from underneath the car. Then she heard the conductor announce, "All aboard for Omaha."

She sat in silence knowing her solitary journey had just begun. After removing her white gloves, she loosened the top blanket surrounding Jimmy Brown, her son, who was only seven days old.

The train moved forward with a sudden jerk, which caused her head to thrust backward as the car began to roll in slow motion. White steam billowed past the windows outside, as she heard a hissing sound as the brakes released on the railroad car. She held Jimmy tightly to her chest. As the train picked up speed, the people on the platform and the countryside became a blur as they sped past.

As she stared out the window, a tear slowly rolled down her cheek and fell onto her navy blue linen skirt. Anyone observing her would wonder why she was crying; why she was going away; and why she was traveling alone. The only way to understand her predicament is to have her tell us her story.

I am the woman on the train, and my name is Georgia Brown. At the age of twenty-eight, I've just had a baby, and I'm heading back home to where I grew up and went to high school in Lexington, Nebraska. It is the middle of March 1940, and I had been living in Kansas City with my sister, Thelma, and her family. Frank, her husband, who is an engineer on the Union Pacific Railroad, allowed me to live with them and their two children, Jean Dell, age six, and Terry, age three, for the past year.

I was in the hospital for five days, and Thelma, who is my older sister, came to visit the baby and me on the second day of my hospital stay while her children were in school. Thelma and I picked out a name that day from the three first names that we both thought would fit this blond-haired baby. The names were Henry, James (our father's name),

William, or Bill. Thelma suggested James Williams, and I liked the sound of it. We both knew that our dad whom we called Papa would be happy to have his name attached to this baby boy. I had been living and working for room and board in an unwed mothers' home for the past six months to be able to afford Jimmy's birth.

Frank, Thelma's husband, gave me a train pass so Jimmy and I could travel to Lexington. I had said my goodbyes to all the other unwed mothers and the employees in the home. I had grown to love each one of them. We had all become mothers to each other as we struggled to have our babies. I stopped at Thelma's to say goodbye to Jean Dell and Terry. Jimmy and I caught a cab and went to the train station.

On the ten-hour train ride to Lexington, I had plenty of time to think about what had happened and what was going to happen in the future. My thoughts were not focused on what had happened in Kansas City. My only concerns were for this little baby boy. Everything that had occurred in the past didn't matter to me. These two beautiful blue eyes and cute small mouth of baby Jimmy drew all my thoughts and my soul to taking care of him and loving him. I had brought him into this world on my own. The only thing that excited me at this time was to show Papa his new grandson. I hoped he would be pleased with such a beautiful boy. Why was I crying? I had to leave Kansas City, which I had grown fond of, with all its exciting and wonderful places to visit. I knew I would miss my sister and her family whom I loved dearly. I had come to Kansas City to begin my life of freedom and to be on my own. I had met a wonderful man, and before he went off to war, I had fallen in love with him.

Before moving to Kansas City, I had grown up in a little town in the middle of Nebraska, located on the Platte River. My family's homestead was a 180-acre farm, seven miles east of Lexington, Nebraska. My mother had gotten sick when I was seven years old, to the point where she was bedridden and couldn't communicate with any of us. My oldest sister had to quit school in seventh grade to take mama's place; trying to raise my two brothers, one older, and one younger than myself.

After I graduated from high school, I took my sister's place at home, for she ran off with a hired hand without giving any notice to anyone. In addition, I had to take care of Papa and my younger brother, Don. Dwight, my older brother, went out on his own and worked as a farmhand for the other farmers in the surrounding countryside. After mother died in November of 1933, I was twenty-three years old, and Papa had moved into town four years earlier. After Momma's death, he allowed me to visit my sister, Thelma, who lived in Kansas City with her husband and two children.

I loved the freedom of Kansas City and asked my sister's husband, Frank, if I could live with them until I got a place of my own, and until I could find a job. I started cleaning houses in the surrounding community two weeks after arriving in Kansas City. After a month, I took the train back to Lexington and told Papa that I was not coming back to Lexington, because I had found a way to make a living and I wanted my freedom.

I didn't want to stay in Lexington to take care of Papa, for I had no money and didn't like asking him for everything that I wanted to buy for myself. Plus, he was very tight with his money. I had done my duty of taking care of the family by washing the clothes, taking care of Mama, and cooking for the three men in our family for four years after I had graduated from high school. Papa understood my feelings. He gave me his blessings to go back to Kansas City, and he saw me off at the train depot.

As I climbed onboard the train, Papa said, "If things don't go right in Kansas City, you can always come back here to Lexington. You will always be my little girl with a big heart."

The ladies of the surrounding neighborhood had contacted Thelma and left me their address to take an interview. I had more interviews, and I chose seven houses to clean when I got back to Kansas City.

Those housekeeping jobs allowed me to pay rent to Thelma's husband, Frank, and I had some money to spend on myself, which I had never had in the past.

Now you might be asking yourself how I got pregnant, and how and why did I have my baby in an unwed mother's home.

This is my love story, which took place in Kansas City in 1939 when the world was on the brink of war. Hitler had demanded the return of colonies for Japan and Italy, and he had warned the U.S. not to meddle in this decision of Hitler's.

One of my jobs was to clean this big, white, framed, two-story house for two redheaded sisters. That house was the first job I found after getting back from Lexington. I found the ad in the *Kansas City Star* newspaper. I had been cleaning their house for a month before I left for Lexington to get my papa's permission to return to Kansas City. I had only been gone for one week and was scheduled to start the following Monday.

On Monday morning, after I got back to Thelma's, I picked up all my cleaning supplies in a tin pail and went over to the sister's house. I started cleaning downstairs after I emptied the trash and swept off the back steps. I climbed the stairs to start cleaning the rooms on the second floor. That's when I noticed a white starched sailor uniform on the floor in the hallway. My first job upstairs was to dust and mop the very shiny hardwood floors in the hallway and the three bedrooms. I squatted down and picked up the white crinkled-up uniform that was in the middle of the hallway floor, and noticed that the soiled uniform had a heavy odor of cigarette smoke.

At that moment, the bedroom door in front of me opened quickly. I was looking down at the uniform in a squatting position, and then I saw two bare feet standing in the doorway. When I stood up, I saw this handsome, blond-haired man standing there with a big smile on his face. His very light blue eyes caught my attention as he stared at me. I noticed that his hair was all messed up, as if he had just awakened from a long night's rest.

He said, "Excuse me, but I don't think we've met. My name is Robert, and I just got in late last night because the train was late getting to town."

He was a well-built man standing there in front of me wearing only his pajama bottoms.

I began to blush and said, "Excuse me!"

I quickly picked up my dust mop, dropped the uniform in front of this man, and went into the bedroom across the upstairs hallway. I started mopping the floor under the bed with hurried strokes.

Later that morning, I was cleaning the kitchen and washing dishes in a suds tub in the sink. Then I would dip the washed dishes in a clean tub of water, which was setting on the countertop. While doing the dishes, I was humming a popular song, which was playing on the radio—a new tune called, "Jeepers Creepers where did you get all those peepers," which made me smile. As soon as the tub was filled with the clean dishes, I placed them on a tea towel to drip-dry before I would stop to dry each dish with another dry towel.

Robert came downstairs stepping lightly until he was right behind me.

He said, "Boo!"

I screamed and jumped about a foot off the floor. Robert caught me in mid-air and gently lowered me to the floor with a soft chuckle. Then I turned around to see who had scared me like that.

Robert said, "I'm sorry, but I've not seen such a pretty girl in the past three months since I've been in the Navy."

He apologized repeatedly as I gained my composure. He then sat down at the kitchen nook and started telling me that I was a pretty girl with funny brown shoes.

He said, "I didn't know my sisters had hired anyone to clean their house."

Robert and I were the only ones in the house because the sisters had gone to work earlier that day. I started to get scared for this was not a place to be with a stranger.

"Say," he said, "what's your name? I need some help around this kitchen."

I said, "Georgia Brown."

He stared at me, and remarked, "You are so cute with your yellow headband wrapped around your hair."

Every once in a while he would turn and ask me another personal question. As we talked, I became less afraid of him because of his conversation.

Then he asked, "Where is the butter located in this kitchen? Someone moved it from where it used to be kept. I used to know where everything was in this kitchen before I went into the Navy."

Of course I didn't answer him, because I didn't live there, and I had no idea where they kept the butter.

He got busy and pulled out the iron skillet, cracked three eggs into it, and fried three eggs over easy.

"Where did my sisters put the toaster?" he asked.

I pointed to the cabinet to the left of the sink. He took out the toaster and popped two pieces of white bread into it. He closed the two little doors, and then he waited until the timer clicked off. As I finished mopping the kitchen floor, he continued talking. He told me that he was home from boot camp and had to go to Chicago for more training before they would ship him out for combat duty. It was close to noon when I finished cleaning the kitchen.

He said, "Georgia, why don't you keep on cleaning, so I'll have somebody to keep me company? Then I can help you clean the house."

"That's kind of you, Robert," I told him. "But I'm finished with my work here, and I have another house to clean this afternoon."

I picked up my cleaning supplies, said goodbye, and walked out the front door. I carried my pail and walked down the street to the second house on the left, where I would begin my cleaning chores in the afternoon.

On the following Monday, I showed up to clean the sisters' house, and Robert was there. Again, he began talking and kidding me all morning as I went around cleaning the house. He followed me from room to room. At the end of the morning, when I was ready to leave for my next job, Robert asked if I would like to see the movie, *Stage Coach* starring John Wayne at the Plaza, which was only four blocks from the house. I did love cowboy movies for they were the movies most shown in Lexington at the downtown theater.

I thought he was very clever and had a great sense of humor. He had me laughing out loud most of the morning as he followed me throughout the house. I was one for fun and laughter, which fit with this sailor, Robert.

Robert said, "I have to leave tomorrow for training, and I won't be back for two months. My training assignment is so top secret that I can't write or make phone calls until I'm finished with my training. Georgia, let's go to the movie tonight and have some fun."

I agreed, and met Robert at the corner that evening at the set time because his sisters' house was on my way to the Plaza—Kansas City's upscale shopping and entertainment area. Robert didn't have a car, so public transportation was the only way around Kansas City. The Plaza was only three blocks away.

Robert said, "I am going to show you a trick about going to the movies here at the Plaza."

One of the tricks to going to the movies at the Plaza was to buy your candy corn popcorn at nine cents a bag at the candy store located next to the movie theater. With the purchase of the candy corn, you still had one cent left over to get some root beer barrel candy. Robert showed me that trick and I never forgot it. Whenever I went to the movies after that night, I always thought of Robert as I got root beer barrels.

I enjoyed the movie, and the walk home was all about his high school and Navy experiences. I did most of the listening and he did the talking. He left me at my front door, which was only two blocks past his sisters' house.

At the door, I said to him, "I really had a good time tonight, and the movie was great. I would like to see you when you return after your training."

Robert didn't try for a kiss but he gently squeezed my hands and came close to me. He gave me a long-lasting hug.

Then he said, "I want to see you when I get back from my training school."

I got back into my daily routine of cleaning houses. When I was cleaning at the redheaded sisters' house, I never gave Robert a second thought. I had decided that he was too busy to remember our last night out together.

One day the oldest sister, Jenny, was home for lunch, and I was finishing up in the kitchen.

Jenny said, "Robert called a couple of days ago and we talked for twenty minutes. At the end of our conversation, he asked if you were still cleaning our house. He asked me to tell you that he will be home in one month for a long leave, and he wants to see you when he comes back. Due to the type of combat training he's doing in Chicago, he's forbidden to write letters to anyone."

Jenny then got up and went out the front door to return to work. I was so happy to hear Robert had remembered me. I flew through the rest of the day cleaning the house next door thinking about Robert. Why would he be interested in me, Georgia Brown? All I knew how to do was clean houses.

On that Saturday when Robert got home from training, the *Kansas City Star* headlines read, "Douglas DC-4 makes first flight from Chicago to New York with forty passengers."

Robert remembered where I lived, and he knocked extra hard on the front door.

Thelma answered the door and this handsome sailor in his dress uniform asked, "Is Georgia Brown at home today?"

Thelma went to the stairs and shouted upstairs, "Georgia, there's a man here to see you, and he's wearing a sailor uniform."

I came bouncing down the stairs, and in my heart, I felt this strange sensation. I was completely surprised to see Robert standing there. He looked so sharp and clean in his white uniform, and both dimples showed off his beautiful smile. He stood there clutching a bouquet of flowers in both hands.

I had quit talking about Robert to Thelma in the last couple of weeks. I thought I would never see Robert again until this morning when I woke up with this sensation in my heart.

He quickly said, "Walk with me to the movies, and we'll see *Robin Hood* with Earl Flynn. He is one of my favorites."

I turned quickly and ran up the stairs, taking them two at a time. I grabbed my new light blue sweater that matched my new blue skirt that I had just bought at the Plaza. I took hold of his arm and pulled him close as we briskly walked down the sidewalk—as if we had known each other for a long time. This time, however, I was doing all the talking and he could do nothing but listen.

We went to see *Robin Hood* and afterward, we sat in the diner and talked, giggled, and laughed about lots of things as we told each other about our lives. Watching his eyes and hand gestures, along with his facial expressions, specific moves and things, tickled me to my heart. Things started to happen to us as we got to know each other with hand touching only, because we were sitting across from each other. We began by sharing the biggest banana split that was on the menu.

After two hours at the diner, Robert got up and moved over to my side of the booth, so he could get closer to me—at my request. I wanted to be closer to his body, and our arms would bump into each other's as we laughed or giggled. I also could tease him about his hair and his small ears. We must have drunk four or five cups of coffee that evening, and we didn't get home until after midnight. The kiss at the door was long and with a lot of meaning. We really liked each other truly from that moment on.

We were inseparable for the next month, because Robert was home only for a month. After that, we didn't know what would happen, because he had been assigned to special combat duty. The headlines in the *Kansas City Star* read, "Czechs collapse: Nazis in Prague."

On the days when I was scheduled to clean the redheaded sisters' house, Robert was always following me from room to room, kidding, and tickling me while I was trying to do my work. There was more kissing and hugging going on than house cleaning. One Monday morning Robert got up early and made breakfast for both of us, knowing that it was my turn to clean their house. We pretended that this was our house and went about making fun as I began to clean around the house. Robert caught me as I was trying to clean the guest bedroom. We fell upon the bed and got into a lover's clutch. I lost control and began to get too excited.

Robert said, "I have to wait until the right time presents itself and today is not the time. You will run out of time."

The next night he whispered in my ear, as we sat watching the movie, *Boys Town* starring Spencer Tracy, "It's time for us to get together and make love. I want you to be with me forever if that's possible."

I took the next morning off, and we went to Robert's house. We made mad passionate love all morning while the sisters were at work. I didn't want to go back to work that afternoon, but Robert insisted that I go. He told me we could continue our lovemaking in the evenings.

The next week before Robert was to leave was the most exciting week I had ever had in my life. We were so in love. The only thing that the two of us could do was to find time and places to make love. I was so in love with him in my whole heart and soul. I loved our time together and couldn't let any of the moments go without Robert, for he was scheduled to leave for duty within days.

The night Robert was scheduled to leave, he said goodbye to his sisters and got in a cab to go to the train station. Robert had the cab driver stop at 4911 Baltimore, where I lived with my sister's family. I had gotten ready to go to the train station with Robert. He wanted me close by his side, because we couldn't get enough of each other. The goodbyes at the train station were one of tears and kisses that would have to last me for my lifetime.

The next month I missed my period, which had not happened to me up to this point in my life. Every Monday when I cleaned the sisters' house, I would look for a letter lying around or in the mailbox, hoping that Robert would have written to his sisters. I had not received any letters or postcards from Robert. I remembered him saying that his instructor had told him that he and all his classmates were not to communicate with anyone about their mission. His instructor had also told him not to call or write letters to anyone.

Nevertheless, I still looked for letters, thinking he would call or drop me a postcard. I met the mail carrier every Monday when he came to deliver the mail around 10:00 a.m. Every time I passed Robert's room, I would get a small pit-a-patter in my heart because of the lovemaking that had taken place in his room. I had such strong memories of each room and of Robert's movements about the house.

I began thinking about what I was going to do when my belly started getting big, and I couldn't conceal my pregnancy. How long could I keep the secret from everyone? I wasn't going to tell anyone until I could decide what I was going to do for money when I had to stop working. That's when I realized that I had to tell my sister, Thelma. I would need help and the only person I knew in Kansas City was her.

After a second month of no period, I decided to tell Thelma. I told her while Jean and Terry left the house to walk to school. I came into the kitchen and sat down at the kitchen table.

I said, "Sister, I want you to come over here and sit down. I have something to tell you."

Thelma pulled up the white wooden chair on the opposite side of the table.

I continued, "I have ten minutes before I have to go to work. You know that I love Robert very much, don't you?"

Thelma said, "I know you two spent a lot of time together when he was home on leave. That's all you talk about is Robert, but I haven't heard you speak of him in the last week or two."

I said, "I've missed my period for two months now and I don't know what to do."

She sat there with her hands crossed in front of her and with her mouth open, as if she was in shock at my last statement.

After a few seconds, she brought her hands up to her face, covered her eyes and cheeks and said, shockingly, "Oh, my God! Oh, my God! This is why Robert was not in your vocabulary around the house this last month."

We started to cry, and she suddenly stood up and came around to my side of the table. As I stood, we hugged each other because of our fear and trepidation of what I would need to do from this point on.

I came up with a lot of ideas and questions such as, "Should we ask Frank if I could stay? Should I go home and live with Papa? Maybe I could earn enough money cleaning houses to get an apartment and keep working to support a babysitter. Maybe I could take the baby with me to the houses while cleaning."

Thelma suggested we both go to Robert's two redheaded sisters and ask if they could or would tell Robert, and get some assistance until he came home.

Crying and trying to figure out the situation, Thelma and I decided to approach the two sisters, who would then let Robert know about my situation. I had not received any letters from Robert to this point in my life. Frank and Thelma didn't have a phone in their house. The only phone I had seen was at the sisters' home. The phone never rang while I was cleaning their house. If the phone had rung while I was there, I would have answered it, hoping that it would be Robert. He knew my work schedule and the days when I cleaned their home.

Thelma had selected a Saturday afternoon and had arranged for the neighbor girl to come over to stay with Jean and Terry while we went to visit the two sisters. Frank was out on assignment with the railroad that Saturday.

Thelma and I had rehearsed and planned for this meeting with the sisters all week. I had mentioned to the sisters the prior Monday that I wanted them to meet Thelma and that we had something important to share with them on Saturday.

Although feeling timid and meek, Thelma and I had gotten enough courage to walk over to the sisters' house. We lightly knocked on their front door. The sisters were home and they invited Thelma and me inside. They ushered us into their parlor, which consisted of a large gray velvet davenport with two large end tables. Lamps with large white, round, shades sat on each table. Across from the coffee table, which sat in front of the davenport were two large gray velvet chairs. Thelma and I sat on the davenport, while the two sisters sat in the chairs opposite us.

The two rather large and tall sisters were very cordial. They offered tea and wheat crackers to Thelma and I as we sank into the davenport. The sisters began to show interest in me for my thoughtfulness at cleaning their house. They became familiar with my personality when Robert and I were around the house in the evenings during the time he was home on leave.

Two of the sisters had been married but the oldest was separated from her husband. The other sister had been divorced for three years. The redheaded sisters were rough with manners and came right to the point when asking their first question.

"Why are the two of you here this afternoon?"

Thelma was the first person chosen last week to explain the situation to the two sisters.

Thelma said, "Georgia and Robert developed a great relationship while Robert was home on leave. It's been two months since Robert went back to the service. We think Georgia is pregnant with Robert's baby, for she has missed two of her periods to this point. We would like you to try to get a hold of Robert to let him know before he goes into combat and can't be reached."

The oldest sister, Jeannie, with the long red hair that hung to her shoulders, stood up, and walked toward Thelma who was taking a sip of her tea.

Jeannie, in her pink-covered open-toed shoes with matching green, floral, patterned dress, which was belted, said, "Robert would not have an affair with Georgia for he's a church-going man."

She turned around and sat in the soft gray chair closest to me. She stared into my eyes, and made me feel very uncomfortable. The second sister, Jane, who was smaller in stature but bigger busted, wore wire rim glasses on her small nose. She, too, stood up and began talking, where her sister had left off. She had her bright red hair pulled up on the top of her head, and it was wrapped in a bun, which was held together with big bobby pins.

She started speaking in a very high tone of voice and pointed to me, saying, "We are not going to tell Robert about any of this conversation. Robert would not have had an affair with you, Georgia, for you're only a cleaning woman."

She then raised both her hands above her head and shouted," I want both of you to leave this house, this moment, and Georgia, you are never to come back to this house again."

Thelma and I jumped up from the davenport with tears in our eyes. We were frightened about what could happen to us at that moment. We picked up our purses, and with long, quick strides, we headed towards the heavy wooden front door. I reached for the doorknob just as Thelma turned around.

She stared at them, and said, "I don't think you are being fair to Georgia and Robert for they are truly in love with each other. I hope your souls will rot in hell."

The two redheaded sisters charged towards Thelma, as she was going through the open front door. The redheaded sisters acted as if they were going to start a fist fight, for they had both their hands in a clutched position in front of them. Thelma closed the wooden door with a heavy slam before the sisters got to the entry hallway.

Thelma's next plan was for me to go back to Lexington to talk with Papa. She told me to buy a wedding ring and tell Papa that I had married Robert before he went off to war, and that we had gone to the Justice of the Peace in Kansas City. Being an unwed mother in Lexington was something I couldn't bring upon my papa and the family.

The second part of the plan was to tell Frank, and ask him if I could stay with Thelma and their family until the baby was born. Then I would go back to Lexington and live with Papa. I was planning to keep cleaning houses until I couldn't continue working. I would give all the money I had earned to Frank for the time I stayed at the house until the baby arrived. After that, I would go back home to Papa.

Frank heard the story and said, "Georgia, I cannot agree with your plan for I am not getting the assignments because of my union. I cannot keep my family and you, too, on the income I am making at this time. I don't know if I can make enough money to pay our house payment and meet the needs of feeding the two children."

He suggested that I look into the unwed mothers' home that was owned by the hospital. He told me to call them, find out the cost of having a baby, and learn how the hospital would handle that cost. I could possibly keep working and then go into the home. After having the baby, then I could go back to Papa—if he would accept my child and me.

I found the address of the Unwed Mother's Home in Kansas City, Kansas. One Saturday, I took the trolley and two buses to the address in the phone book. I talked to the superintendent of the home and got all the information I needed. Then I filled out the application and took a tour of the home. They told me that I could go to work at the home right away. I would be cleaning and helping other unwed mothers to take care of their clothing. I would also help with meals until I had to stop to have my own baby. Doing this work in the home, I would not have to pay the costs of having my baby.

I was excited when I told Frank and Thelma my news that evening at the dinner table. Frank then said that Thelma and I should go together to Papa's to see if we could get his approval. Thelma arranged to have the neighbors take care of the kids while we were gone. Frank got two train passes for the next weekend.

The ten-hour train ride from Kansas City to Lexington was very stressful for both of us. Thelma told me that Papa wasn't speaking to her, and that he'd be upset. He wouldn't want anything to do with her because she had run off and left him to care for the family by himself. Papa was still upset about Thelma running off with Frank. We were so frightened that Papa would not want to listen to our problems and would turn us away. Besides that, we wondered how we would handle the townspeople and the rumors that I was unwed and expecting a child.

Thelma and I talked and cried the whole ten hours on our train trip. We discussed how to approach Papa and we talked about the words we would say to him when we got to his house. I was rehearsing the things to say and Thelma was role-playing Papa's part. We decided that Thelma would speak at specific times, and I would try to explain to Papa the reasons for everything.

Papa met us at the station because we had called him from the train station in Omaha, when we switched trains. Papa had a phone at the harness shop, which he operated in Lexington, and that was the only way to contact him. None of the townspeople or relatives knew we were coming.

Papa met us at the station that bright and sunny Saturday morning, and he drove us to his house. Thelma and I made breakfast in Papa's small kitchen, and then all three of us sat around the kitchen table for breakfast. The house looked the same as it did when I left a year ago—everything was in the same place except for the dust on top of every piece of furniture. I started out by telling Papa about the house cleaning jobs and the different people who owned the houses. Thelma had brought some pictures of Jean Dell and Terry with news about their school and music lessons. She also showed him pictures of the house Frank and Thelma had just bought and described the work Frank was doing at the railroad.

Without notice, Papa turned toward me and asked, "Have you met any interesting men, Georgia?"

I saw an opening at that moment and told Papa the whole story about Robert and his two redheaded sisters.

"Papa, the two sisters' house that I was cleaning," I began, "they had a brother who was in the Navy. I met him while he was on leave."

This speech wasn't in the rehearsed plan that Thelma and I had constructed.

Then I said, "His name is Robert. He and I started dating and I fell in love with him. He is a wonderful person, and I felt so empty when he left. Now he's gone to combat training and he was instructed not to communicate with the sisters or myself."

I tried to explain the feelings I had for Robert.

"Papa, I love him with all my heart and soul, and I know he loves me."

Without hesitating, I kept talking, "Papa, I have missed my period for two months."

That statement was another embarrassing part for me. I had never talked to Papa about sex when I was a child, let alone now. That subject was for girls only and Mama was the one who handled the sex subjects.

I didn't tell Papa the part about our meeting with the two redheaded sisters. Thelma kicked me under the table when I starting getting to that part of the conversation. I went to the next subject of the Unwed Mothers' Home.

"Papa, I want to go back to Kansas City and work until it is time for my baby's birth, and I don't want to be a burden to anyone."

Then I stopped talking, and there was a pause for a few long seconds. Thelma placed her fork down on her plate, where she had been pushing her eggs around for several minutes. We both stared at Papa.

Then, as rehearsed, Thelma said, "Papa, could you help Georgia after the baby comes? She wants to come home and live with you."

Papa could see tears welling up in both his daughters' eyes. They looked scared, and stared at the flower pattern on the vinyl tablecloth. He looked at both of his daughters, and until this point, he had said nothing.

Then, speaking very softly, while looking at me, he said, "Georgia, you will have no money, and this man Robert will not help, for he is not writing or contacting you. So, he is of no help. Frank and Thelma have their own life to deal with, and they can't help you. The only thing is that we must keep this as one big secret and tell everyone that you are married to Robert. That's the only choice you have, Georgia."

He stopped and put both his elbows on the table. He placed his palms together in front of his face, and bent all his fingers inward to make a shelf for his chin to rest upon. Thelma and I had seen this posture only once or twice before, and only when Papa was making decisions that were very important for the family.

He continued, "You will have to get a wedding band and come home with your baby. The townspeople will not find out about your situation, because that would be a horrible thing here in Lexington. The three of us must work out all the details and not let any of the other family members know about our plan."

Thelma and I had tears streaming down our cheeks, and Papa was saying this as tears started coming down his cheeks, also. He stood up, came around the table, and took both of us girls into his arms as we stood up. We both hugged him and began bawling out loud and kissing our daddy repeatedly. This had not happened since the day Della, his wife, and Papa had gotten back home with the diagnosis of our mom having Huntington Chorea disease.

The girls never saw their dad cry, even at Della's funeral. He didn't show an outbreak of any emotions. He had gone through a lot of tragedies in his life, but he never complained to his family about any hardships. He just accepted what he had to do to get to this time of his life.

So here I am sitting on the train going to Lexington with my darling son, Jimmy Brown. I am going back to live with Papa and again be under his realm where he dictates what clothing and things I can purchase, for I have no other choice. The reason I am crying is for fear of how my old classmates and the community will act towards me if they find out that I had Jimmy out of wedlock. The small-town mentality and the church's doctrines frown upon sinners who have children out of wedlock. Papa and I would have to live a lie to keep people from knowing the truth about Robert.

Papa had purchased a harness shop in downtown Lexington with the money he made from the sale of his first house. That was the house where my brother Don lived with Papa after Mama died in November of 1933. Papa was now living in his mother's house at the north end of Lexington. Papa worked in his harness shop all day except for his noon-hour break, when he drove home for lunch and a nap. He was now sixty-eight years old and starting a new venture to earn money.

I was again in the position of cooking and cleaning Papa's house as I took care of baby Jimmy. I was very content with the situation, and I caught myself humming tunes as I used to when I was a kid. I loved the tune, "Jimmy Crack Corn" and I would break out in verse some days while working around the house. Other days while I bathed Jimmy, I sang children songs, like, "Twinkle, Twinkle Little Star" and others songs I remembered. I sang all those songs to my darling Jimmy. I loved to talk to Jimmy for I knew he was listening to every word. Jimmy's gaze would follow me as I moved around the house. I loved to put him in the baby booster seat that Papa had made for Jimmy out of materials he had found at the shop.

The only thing I didn't like was the distance between Papa's house and the town, since it was too far for me to walk. I couldn't carry Jimmy and the groceries, because Papa had not bought a baby buggy. Every evening after work, Papa would have to bring home all the groceries and other things I needed. I was housebound and had no one to talk to, because Papa didn't have a phone. The only people I could speak with were relatives or Papa's friends who dropped over to play cards in the evenings.

Baby Jimmy got all the attention as he grew from being entertained, hugged and cuddled by me. I loved him more and more each day, for he loved to laugh and coo when I tickled him. Papa and Jimmy became good pals. Jimmy knew Papa's voice when he came home for lunch or when he got home from work in the evening. Jimmy would kick and squeal from his crib when he heard Papa coming into the house. Papa loved to tickle Jimmy and it made him smile with delight. Jimmy moved his little arms to grab Papa's finger, and tried to stick Papa's finger in his little drooling mouth.

Papa started noticing that my mood changed because I had no one to communicate with except for Jimmy. I thought I was content by not letting my classmate friends know that I was in town. I was in the house most of the day taking care of my sweet Jimmy. Papa suggested that I start getting involved in church activities as I used to teach a Sunday school class and participated in the choir when I was in high school. The church was only four blocks from the house. I could pull Jimmy in the little red wagon if I wasn't too embarrassed because we didn't have a baby buggy yet.

Jimmy and I started going to church on Sunday with Papa. I got involved in conversations with old acquaintances on the church steps after the sermons. I learned there was a group of mothers whose husbands were serving in the service. Those women would meet on Wednesday afternoons to help with different projects for the church.

I left little Jimmy with the neighbor next door and attended a couple of meetings. I found out that I had to explain what happened to my husband who was serving in the war. When people asked which island he was located on, or which ship he was associated with, I couldn't answer those questions. I didn't feel comfortable telling lies, and trying to make a conversation just wasn't in my heart. I stopped going to those functions because of that fact.

When I met some of my high school chums, things had changed, and they all had their own families. I didn't fit in with them since I was a mother with a husband overseas. Some evenings my friends would invite me over to play cards with them and their husbands. I found that being pretty and single, and with a husband overseas, I became a threat to some of my old girlfriends, because their husbands tried to flirt with me. Every time my friends invited me over for the evening to play card games, I tried to ignore their husbands, who were out of line. I sometimes never got invited a second time, and my friends never gave a reason why they didn't invite me back.

Three months after Jimmy and I came to live with Papa, he would come home for lunch in the afternoons and the house was in the same condition as it was when he had left that morning. Breakfast dishes were still in the sink; the drip pan under the icebox was overflowing, and the laundry was piled up out on the porch. Sometimes, I would be napping with Jimmy when Papa arrived home for lunch. He would make his own lunch and be out of the house before Jimmy would stir and wake me from a sound sleep. Papa noticed I was not going to Wednesday afternoon luncheons, or to the women's functions. My excuse was that I was feeling tired after staying up all night with Jimmy. Some days I wouldn't even feel like talking to Papa, because I was feeling sad and lonely. Most days I was more into Jimmy's care and not doing much around the house when Papa was at work.

After work in the evenings, Papa would look at properties in downtown neighborhoods. He figured that if I could get out of the house with the baby buggy and do my own shopping, I could also visit some of my friends for coffee downtown. Papa wanted me to get back to being myself again.

Papa found a new house, which was only four blocks from downtown. The house had one big bedroom, and Papa said he could divide it into two bedrooms. It had a large living room, and a dining room that was combined with a small kitchen that was close to the dining area. Off to the side of the kitchen was a screened-in porch, which could serve as the laundry room. The inside walls were made of tongue-and-groove pine wood board, which were stained dark brown.

The floors throughout the house were covered with linoleum that had small yellow flowers.

Jimmy and I moved into the new house. After settling in with our old furniture and moving from a big kitchen into a small kitchen, I was excited because I made room for a play area for Jimmy on the porch.

Papa bought a new dark blue cloth baby buggy with big chrome wheels. I could put Jimmy in the buggy and walk to the downtown area. I would buy my own groceries and other things that we needed for Jimmy. The budget that Papa gave me let me have my freedom again. I began taking walks downtown every morning after I had gotten Papa out of the house for his workday. I would hurry to get Jimmy bathed, and I'd dress him in a nice outfit that I had found on one of my shopping outings. I would then clean the breakfast dishes, empty the icebox drip pan, and make sandwiches and a thermos full of coffee to take to Papa's shop for his lunch. My heart began to sing again, because of all the things I could do that were fun for Jimmy and me.

I started meeting my old friends again on the streets and they would all stop and admire Jimmy. Several friends sometimes stopped, and we would have coffee at the corner drugstore on Washington and 5th Street.

The minister, Mr. Charles, walked into my classroom one Sunday after I had finished teaching my Sunday school class. He asked me to follow him to his office because he said he wanted to talk to me. I picked up Jimmy and carried him into the minister's office, and we sat down.

I asked, "What is it you want to talk to me about, Mr. Charles?"

He replied, "We are pleased with what you are doing with the young children, but we have had a couple of complaints from the mothers. They have approached me and suggested that you shouldn't teach the Sunday school class."

I said, "I haven't offended the children, and they seem to like the stories that we get our lessons from."

Mr. Charles said, "You're doing a fine job teaching, but the mothers think there is no reason for Jimmy to be in the class. They think he is a disruption to your lessons. Therefore, I am giving your class to Mrs. Olson as of next Sunday. We will no longer need your services."

I just stood there dumbfounded. I didn't know what to say. So, I nodded, as an acknowledgment that I had heard what he said. I turned and left his office feeling somewhat angry, disappointed, and frustrated.

Again, I thought, *people are rejecting me because of Jimmy. I thought their hearts were bigger than that."*

Jimmy and I went home that Sunday morning to discuss the situation with Papa.

Papa said, "I am very upset that Mr. Charles told you not to come back to teach your Sunday school class. If you want to pursue teaching the Sunday school class, I will talk to Mr. Charles for you. I can bring Jimmy home with me after the morning service, which would allow you to teach Sunday school."

I felt there was some other reason Mr. Charles hadn't mentioned, but I didn't want to say anything to Papa or pursue it with Mr. Charles, since he was the minister. I had noticed that many of the parishioners were not speaking to me, as they had done when I first became involved with the church again.

A couple weeks later while I was pushing Jimmy and the carriage, we were on our way to Papa's store. I saw one of my school friends hurriedly crossing the street in the middle of the block. She was trying to avoid Jimmy and me when she saw us coming her way. I didn't think much of it until a couple of days later. That's when I noticed that other people were avoiding me in the stores.

I loved taking Jimmy out and showing him off, because he was walking now. Sometimes he would hang onto the buggy as we walked towards town. Sometimes he and I would walk out the front door of the house and turn left to go to the little Huff's Stop & Shop store, which was their living room converted into a small store, just to get Jimmy a little ice cream. Mrs. Huff loved to see us coming because she adored little Jimmy and always made a fuss over him. When we would go to the shop for lunch with Papa, we always had to stop next door at the Hess' creamery. Jimmy loved Mrs. Hess because she would pick him up, hug, and kiss him. He returned the hugs and kisses to her.

Sometimes for lunch, Papa would take us to the Haggardon Café, located across the street and down on the corner of Main Street. Wally Haggardon would always make a big fuss over Jimmy. At the end of our lunch, Wally, whom I went to high school with, would bring out a little dish of bread pudding with whipped cream on the top. Wally would dip his little finger into the whipped cream and put a dab of it on Jimmy's little nose. They both would laugh out loud.

Jimmy was so tickled, and every time we turned the corner to go to Papa's store, he would say, "Wally, Wally" in his little voice.

Then I would say, "Yes, that's where he works."

One day, I tripped on the front step while bringing two quart-sized bottles full of milk that the milkman had delivered to our front door that morning. In my fall, I turned and landed on my backside, but I still held onto the two milk bottles, and they didn't break. I never mentioned the incidents of falling to Papa.

That day, I had too much work to do to think about the milk incident. I tried to get all of my work done so I could go to Papa's store and take him some sandwiches for lunch. At the end of the day, before I dropped off to sleep, I began to think those incidents of falling and dropping things had happened to my mother when we first noticed the changes in her. I didn't have time to worry about my clumsiness, and I put the thoughts out of my mind.

Jimmy was my main concern, yet I wondered why my friends were avoiding me when I went downtown. I also noticed in the last couple weeks that none of my friends invited me to card games anymore.

Maybe my secret was out about having no husband, but since I hadn't told anyone the truth, I just figured it was their own gossip they were spreading. Apparently, they had to make up a story to suit their curiosity.

To me, none of that mattered because I had what was most important, which was my son, Jimmy, whom I loved. He was the joy of my life and would always be the center of my world.

But in the back of my mind, I wondered if some of my symptoms were similar to my mother's illness, which the doctors said was known as St. Vitus Dance or Huntington's Chorea disease.

Chapter 2

Georgia Searches for Answers

To satisfy her curiosity about the symptoms of Huntington's Chorea, Georgia Brown went to the library to research the disease.

Georgia was seated at the research librarian's desk, and she was anxious to read whatever materials were available.

The research librarian returned to her desk, but she didn't have any books in her hands.

"I'm sorry, Miss Brown, but I couldn't locate any reference materials for Huntington's Chorea or St. Vitus Dance disease."

Georgia closed her eyes and took in a deep breath. It was apparent she was disappointed.

"Thank you," Georgia said. "Yes, thank you for your time."

With a forlorn look on her face, Georgia left the library and walked straight home without stopping in any of the shops.

When I got home, I decided to write a letter to my Uncle Frank Culver, because his wife, Georgia, whom I was named after, had been diagnosed with the disease when I was taking care of my mother. About a week later, I received a big package in the mail from Uncle Frank. It contained a lot of literature he had gathered on St. Vitus dance.

I immediately sat on the couch and read every bit of information he had sent. I learned that the symptoms of this devastating disease usually didn't show up until after the age of thirty-five. It was reported that one of the first observable symptoms is clumsiness, and as the disease progresses, movements could become uncontrollable.

I was alarmed and wondered how this might affect my ability to take care of Jimmy. I was frightened to read more, yet fearful that if I didn't, I would just be postponing the inevitable. So I continued reading the materials Uncle Frank had sent.

I found two articles that were cut out of medical journals, stating that the disease included other symptoms, such as forgetfulness, irritability, and withdrawal—in the early stages — progressing to dementia with severe memory loss and lack of reasoning. My mother had acquired these symptoms while I was growing up. Once the illness was diagnosed, the article stated, it could continue relentlessly for ten to twenty years, and heart disease was the most common cause of death, preceded by illness, falls, choking, and dementia.

Tears fell from my eyes and I began to tremble. All I could think was, *Jimmy. My poor little baby, Jimmy. What will happen to you?*

Two hours later, I began my regular routine of getting ready for our daily walk to downtown. I had taken care of the block of ice that the iceman had delivered to the back door. I placed a small block of ice into the top cabinet of the icebox. Then I emptied the drip pan underneath the icebox. I continued with the process of putting away the breakfast dishes that I had just finished washing. While I put the glasses and dishes in the overhead kitchen cabinets, I accidently bumped into the top shelf and dropped all three glasses that I had in my hand. When the glasses hit the flowered pattern linoleum floor, the glasses shattered into a million pieces. I reached for the dustpan and long-handled broom from beside the icebox and swept up the broken glass. I was glad Jimmy was in his bassinet in the other room. Otherwise, the incident could have been devastating with all the flying slivers of glass.

Later that morning, I stopped at the five-and-dime store and picked up a box of six new glasses. Papa came home for lunch and saw the glasses on the kitchen table.

He asked, "Why are there new glasses here on the table?"

I explained, "I needed more glasses because I broke several of them this morning while trying to put them back in the cabinet."

That was the end of our conversation.

A week later, I was outside on the porch washing clothes in the washing machine, which had an agitator and a ringer. The clothes would slosh back and forth in the hot sudsy water, propelled by the agitator's blades. While holding a short broomstick in my hand, I would pick up the hot, wet clothing with the short broomstick and guide each garment into the ringer, which was located at the back of the tub. The clothing would be squeezed between two rubber rollers and then it would fall into the round tin washtub, which I had set on a three-legged stool at the back of the machine. The water from the squeezed clothing ran back into the tub where the agitators were moving back and forth.

I turned the agitator knob located on the side of the washing machine to the off-position. Next, I pulled the drain hose off the opposite side of the tub. Then I placed the hose into another tin washtub that was on the floor next to the washing machine to catch all the dirty drain water. I was in the process of turning around when something happened. I stepped wrong and fell sideways over the washtub that was on the floor. I hit my head on the side of the tub as I fell, and I landed on the floor next to the tin washtub.

Getting up slowly, the only damage I could find was a bruised knee. I picked up the washtub full of wet clothing and carried it out the back door. I began to hang the clothes and sheets on the wire line that hung between two T-shaped poles that spanned the length of the backyard. I wore a clothespin apron filled with clothespins, and I pinned the damp washed clothing and sheets to the wire. The hot summer winds would blow the clothing dry.

By late fall of that year, Jimmy was beginning to walk, and he held onto furniture as he maneuvered his way around the house. I was concerned for Jimmy's safety, and I moved everything small up higher to keep it out of little Jimmy's reach. I noticed I was now forgetting little things, such as buying grocery items, which I knew we needed, so I vowed to write everything down. Unfortunately, I sometimes forgot to take the list with me when I went shopping.

Papa began finding various stacks of lists located throughout the house in odd places. He also noticed that I was not keeping the house as clean as I had normally done in the past. I would usually do my heavy cleaning on Mondays and Thursdays, but lately I couldn't even remember what day it was. I had also begun to stack clothes on the ironing board that I intended to iron. However, there were so many clothes piled on top of it that Papa couldn't even see its surface.

One day I went shopping and Papa questioned me about why my lipstick was not quite square on my lips. I got very offended and went into a tizzy over his comments. I wiped the red lipstick off on the sleeve of my blouse. It didn't take long for me to realize that I was getting more aggravated over little things that normally wouldn't bother me at all. I started noticing that I was getting more bruises on my legs and hips from hitting the furniture around the house. At first, I thought I was hurrying too quickly to get all my chores finished. Then I noticed those little accidents in my life reminded me of my mother, Della. Her illness started with her being very clumsy around the house.

At the age of twelve, I was the youngest daughter of the family. I was my mother's favorite child. We were emotionally tied because of our similar personalities. Growing up, I had the best of both worlds, since my oldest sister, Thelma, looked after me while at school. She also taught me a lot about things girls need to know.

She taught me how to dress my dolls with corn silk and cornhusks because they made such fancy dresses. She showed me how to make fancy dough to bake special cookies, and we made cakes with cinnamon and sugar frosting. She taught me how to skip rope on the front porch. We played jacks on the kitchen floor, because the linoleum surface allowed us to swoop up the five to seven jacks in one sweep, while catching the ball on one bounce.

My mother, Della, was a school teacher and at one time, she taught me how to think out problems before I took action to solve the problem. She coached me on the proper position of holding my head and shoulders while attending church and school functions. She told me it gave me a personal presentation, as she called it. I was very graceful and knew how to handle myself at social functions. Thelma and my brothers Dwight and Don had me doing summersaults and performing riding tricks on horses. Don and I did acrobatics, and we gave horse-riding performances for neighbors and friends on Sunday afternoons in the Brown's front yard.

I began to notice little things happening to our mother while she was cooking. The kitchen table was where I would do my homework. My household duties were to set the table and fetch the water pitcher. I would fill all the glasses with a pitcher of water that came from the hand pump by the sink. On a couple of occasions, Della would try to retrieve the salt shaker above the stove, but she would drop the shaker before coming back to the table.

Sometimes Della would drop the round iron stove lid as she lifted it using the poker handle from the top of the stove to check the fire beneath the lid. Lifting and dropping the iron lid from the poker handle by accident would make a clanging noise as it hit the iron stove. Then it rolled and created a vibrating sound as it hit the stovetop. The lid kept spinning around in circles as it came to rest on top of the stove. These and other little things that were happening were not like what our mother would usually do while working in the kitchen.

When Della was out of the kitchen getting something from the cellar or looking after Don, Thelma and I would discuss the ever-evolving changes happening to her.

Thelma would say, "Why is Mother bumping into the chairs around the kitchen table so often and knocking things over? She didn't do that before, either."

I said, "I've noticed that Mama gets angry at us over little things, like the time I splashed water on you while I was washing dishes the other night. It's not like her to jump on me. Usually she would never speak to anyone in harsh tones."

Later that night Della told me, "I'm sorry for speaking to you in such a sharp, out-of-control manner."

One of the special times I loved was when Mama would braid my hair in the evenings after my bath. Sometimes she would talk about a certain topic, but when she'd try to say a word, she couldn't say it.

She would say, "Georgia, what word am I looking for?"

Then I would give her the word or sentence structure. I noticed Mama was missing conversational words, and she'd never done that before.

Within the next year, Thelma was now braiding by hair instead of Mama for there would be days when Mama wouldn't get out of bed because she was feeling very tired. That began happening once or twice a week, and everyone was concerned. The children started asking Papa what was wrong with Mama.

Papa had the local doctor come to the house to look at Mama. He reported that she had a virus that was going around the neighborhood. Not all the medicines that the doctor left at the house would help

Mama's tired feeling. Papa was getting concerned because of the effects on the household chores and responsibilities.

The doctor suggested that he should take Della to a specialist in Grand Island. The next week Dwight hooked up the team of horses to the buckboard wagon. He drove the team of horses and took Papa and Della to town, which was thirteen miles from the farm. Papa and Mama boarded the train to Grand Island, which was an all-day trip. The rest of the day, Dwight stayed in town to wait for the folks to return on the train that evening.

My mother was very close to her sister, Georgia, and she wrote her a letter once a week. Georgia and her husband, Frank Culver, lived in Oakfield, Wisconsin. My mother named me after my Aunt Georgia. She was a few years older than Della, and she had experienced similar symptoms a couple of years prior to Della's illness. Frank Culver was very concerned and had taken Aunt Georgia to a specialist in Chicago two months before Papa and Della went to Grand Island. In the last letter from Georgia Culver, the diagnosis was Huntington's Chorea, and they didn't have much knowledge or medical research information on the subject.

While in Grand Island, Papa called Frank Culver from the specialist's office at the suggestion of the doctor. The Grand Island doctor got the phone number of the specialist in Chicago and confirmed that Della had the same symptoms as her sister.

When my family heard that Mama had Huntington's Chorea, we wanted to know how it affected the people who had it. We wanted to know what was going to happen to her and to us.

The next day Papa and Della had all the children gather together in the living room so he could talk to us about Mama and her illness. He shared information that the doctor had given them, which they had read on their return train ride from Grand Island.

Mama was strong, but I noticed her hands trembling as she spoke to us. She told the family she would be changing from day to day, and it would depend upon different things and stresses she was going through mentally. When asked, the children stated that they had noticed some of the changes in Mama's behavior.

Mama spoke up and said, "This disease is a progressive disease, which means I will get worse as time goes on. Papa and I want you to know that we love you children, no matter what might happen."

Papa knew that things would be changing for us kids, and he said, "I would like to have all of you pitch in and help me take care of your mama. There will be days when she will be so tired that she won't be able to do anything, including dressing and feeding herself. Then there will be some days she will act and feel like nothing's happened."

Mama cut into the conversation, and said, "Please help me as much as you can on my off-days."

Papa was concerned about Della, since it wasn't safe for her to be cooking or around the stove during the next couple of weeks. Della began falling for no reason at all. Her muscles would give way without notice, and she would suddenly land on the floor. Mama got to the point where she couldn't take care of her hair or dress herself on those bad days. Some days she would just sit and stare into space, not knowing what was going on around her. Because of all this, everyone had to change their schedules to keep the household stable.

Papa and Dwight took care of the farm chores and crops. Don and Georgia were to take care of the hen house and feeding the chickens as well as gathering the eggs. Don was instructed to help Thelma clean up after meals.

Thelma had to quit school and stay home to cook and wash the clothes and linens, which there were a lot of because of Mama. Keeping Mama clean and in diapers was Georgia and Thelma's responsibility, which resulted in at least four to five changes a day. Since Thelma was the only one home during the day, she had the task of taking Mama out of bed and putting her into the big chair after naps.

On Mama's bad days, she couldn't stand up. She also fought with anyone if they tried to move her from the bed to her chair or vice versa. Dwight or Papa would have to be called out in the fields sometimes. We'd have to go outside on the front porch and ring the big bell on the post, signaling for them to come home to help us move Mama.

My relationship with Mama changed after the Grand Island visit. She took me in the bedroom later that day and told me that when she had good days, she wanted to express her feelings and emotions to me. She wanted me to tell the other children and Papa how she felt, including the things that she thought needed to be addressed among the whole family. I reassured her that we would help to calm her fears and misunderstandings.

Don and I attended school everyday, but I had to be home as soon as school was out to help with the chores of taking care of Mama. The first chore was to take down the clothing and sheets from the clothesline. Ironing was another chore, along with setting the table for dinner. I was instructed to sit with Mama in her bedroom to keep her company by reading to her or going over my lessons. Some days, Mama needed help getting to the bathroom and walking to the kitchen to be near Thelma. Mama could only sit in the kitchen chair for short periods due to the shaking and uncontrolled movements her body was going through. This would exhaust Mama's energy to the point where she had to get to bed with the help of her children.

Mama's uncontrollable arm movements on bad days would get to the point where she couldn't hold a spoon. Then Thelma or I would have to feed her. Mama sometimes had trouble swallowing—even little piece of potatoes—and we had to serve only mashed potatoes. From there on, we would cut her food up very fine. Then she could swallow without difficulty. Some days one of the girls would have to hold Mamma's head still with both hands, and the other girl would place the food in Mama's mouth with a spoon.

Mama started getting her arms and legs into bizarre body positions because of the uncontrolled movements. Thelma and I kept a close watch on her, and we were always trying to straighten out her arms or legs by pulling on them and tying them to the bed with old pillowcases and safety pins. Mama's mind would sometimes be very down, and she would stare into space. On other days, her memory would fade slowly. It wasn't unusual for her not to recognize her neighbors or friends who came to visit.

Mama would have days where she didn't shake, and her mind was as clear as if nothing had happened. She would get out of her bed and could walk to the bathroom. As the day wore on, her strength would start to falter and her shaking would become so severe that she would have to get back into bed or just sit in her big easy chair. On those good days, I would come home from school, and we would talk about all of our feelings.

One day Mama said, "On some days, I can start my day doing very well, but then something happens that irritates me. One of my biggest irritations is trying to get anyone in the family to understand what I want that would make my day easier. My throat and my tongue seem as if they're not communicating with each other. That is why I end up doing a lot of grunts and gyrations to get somebody to understand what I want. I can't control my emotions, so I become enraged with anger, and that's when I start screaming and crying."

Mama told me, "That's why I don't even try to communicate when those spasms come over me. I'm irritated with my inability to control many of these situations. My sensitivity meter just seems to kick into overdrive. I'll feel angry and then for no reason, I'll go into a rage. I start throwing and ripping my bed clothing or anything I can get hold of to toss across the room. This comes out of my rage."

According to Mama, to contain her irritation, she had to stop it before it got out of hand.

Mama said, "I can't control this flood of emotions. After I explode, then I feel like I need to apologize for my ugly behavior. It makes me feel horrible for treating my loved ones the way I do during those moments."

She told us that self-control was another thing people lose when they have Huntington's Chorea.

She said, "Sometimes I have an overwhelming desire to destroy something when I feel rage taking over my body. I feel out of control."

When Mama felt her irritation starting to build, she would start to swear like a sailor, while trying to verbalize what was happening. The first time this occurred, the whole family couldn't believe Mama could say such words, and it was even more amazing she knew those swear words. Trying to tell someone with Huntington's Chorea to stop being angry or suggesting they discuss their overreaction, didn't work, as Thelma and I found out.

Over time, we learned that Mama needed a lot of rest. Her daily nap in the morning and again in the afternoon was essential. We had to make sure she didn't overdo it in the energy department when she was feeling good. We had to keep her from exerting too much physical energy. We also had to make sure she ate regularly and avoided overheating her body with too much clothing or bedding while she was in bed.

Before being diagnosed with Huntington's Chorea, Mama would go out with our family to public school functions as well as church sermons every Sunday. Now she was embarrassed because of her uncontrolled body movements. Within the next two or three months, her shaking and rhythmic arms and legs would get out of control and she worried about embarrassing the family or herself.

Mama said, "When I embarrass myself or others in public, the flight-or-fight response is activated. When I become angry, I burst into tears, and I want to run for the hills, panic, or freeze up. I know now that's why you don't take me to public places anymore."

Groups of people would frighten Mama because there was too much stimulation with everybody talking, and the noise level was too high for her. She told me she couldn't control her thought processes to separate the different conversations. This would make her brain shut down, and she'd end up staring into space, which embarrassed everyone concerned.

One bright afternoon in the spring, Mama told me she loved her big soft chair in the bedroom. She could look outside and see that the trees were budding, the birds were chirping, and the sun warmed her soft face. She loved moments like these, since the sun kept her nice and cozy warm. Her shaking was under control, and the only thing moving was her right foot, which she had crossed over her left leg. Both of her legs were resting on a big pillow on the floor. The reason she liked the big chair was also because it was soft and deep, and it absorbed her body's back-and-forth motion as it tremored throughout the day.

Mama wanted to sit with Thelma after breakfast, however, bad things started to happen when she sat on the wooden chair in the kitchen. Mama had to fight the tremors and uncontrolled arm movements while trying to hold her body from sliding off the chair. Her muscles didn't have the same strength as they used to have. She collapsed when she sat or stood in one place for too long. Thelma would look for clues as Mama sat there in the kitchen. As soon as Thelma saw Mama fading, she would take her back to bed for her morning nap.

When Mama's body was overheated, it set off her irritability in a short amount of time. Blankets and comforters had to be taken off immediately because Mama had become a human radiator. The constant muscle trembling added a few degrees to her body temperature.

As Mama's condition worsened, we agreed to implement silent signals as a way for her to let us know when she wanted her visitors to leave. When company came over, one of the girls would sit real close to Mama. When Mama's anxiety levels began to rise, she would touch one of us on the arm, which signaled that she wanted us to take over the conversation and start making excuses. The visitors were told that Mama was getting tired and it was time for them to leave.

Sometimes Mama would tug on her earlobe to signal it was time to get back to her big chair. From across the room, Papa would scratch his nose, which was a signal to Mama, asking if she was all right. Mama could shake her head yes or no depending upon what action she wanted—to stay up or to lie down and rest.

Mama always worried when someone would ask her an open-ended question. She would try to answer the question, but she would lose her train of thought. Suddenly her words wouldn't make sense, and she would end up talking about a completely different topic. When that happened, Mama would put her palms together, which was the sign for Thelma or I to take over the conversation. Mama appreciated this, since sometimes she felt like a real bore when she had to answer questions.

After experiencing many of the symptoms common to Huntington's Chorea, I became deeply disturbed about my physical and mental condition. It reminded me of what my mother had gone through when I was a little girl. My moods spiraled further downward as I contemplated Jimmy's future without me being around. I would talk to Jimmy as he walked and climbed around the house exploring furniture, and opening and closing drawers and doors. I would tell Jimmy how much I loved him as I entertained him.

On this specific day, I sat down and wrote a short letter to Thelma and her family, using the stationery that I kept in the top drawer of my dresser. I began thinking that things were not going right, and I had to let Jimmy know how much I loved him. Throughout the next few weeks, I wrote letters to Jimmy and placed them in various dresser drawers underneath the clothing where no one could find them. I knew that someday Jimmy would go through those drawers. When he was older and would read the letters, he would understand my love for him. He was so lovable, and he loved to climb up on my lap and hug my neck.

He would say, "Kiss, kiss."

I also started hiding things throughout the house. One day, Papa found his precious silver dollars in the breadbox while he was making Sunday breakfast. Another time he found some of my jewelry in the flour bin. I became obsessed with saving things.

Papa recognized the signs of Della's disease happening to me, but he thought the symptoms would go away. He reasoned that I was too young at the age of twenty-eight to have this dreadful disease.

From Uncle Frank's research materials, I learned more about Huntington's Chorea disease. Patients suffering from St. Vitus dance, or Huntington's Chorea disease as it was called twenty years later, showed degenerative changes in the basal ganglia structures, which ultimately resulted in a severely shrunken brain and enlarged ventricles. The caudate and putamen brain structures are particularly affected as they shrink to half their normal size.

Within the next month or two, I started showing signs of not wanting to be around loud sounds or bright lights. The sound of the radio sometimes got to me, and I would have to turn the volume down, because it made me nervous. I would want to sit in Papa's soft chair and pull my knees to my chest. I would just sit there and stare at the wall until I realized the noise of the radio was my problem.

When I went downtown and many people were talking in a group, the sounds became garbled, and it irritated me. I would lose control of my ability to separate different conversations. I would become very quiet and wouldn't participate in any discussions, and that made me feel very embarrassed to be around a lot of people. This only happened once or twice a week, but previously, I had never noticed the strange behaviors that affected my personality. My hands would start to tremor slightly when I was in too much of a hurry or under stress.

Some days when I had been sitting at a table for a long time, I noticed that when I stood up to get ready to leave, I had a hard time taking that first step, which had never happened to me before. I was bumping into a lot of furniture and had many bruises on my legs and on my right shoulder. I always seemed to get these bruises when I approached the entry way into the kitchen. The problem was with either my eyesight or my inability to judge distances. I really began to get scared that something drastic was going to happen to me.

One evening at the dinner table, I was so concerned that I started discussing my fears with Papa.

First, I placed his favorite bread pudding dessert in front of him, and then I asked, "What's going to happen to Jimmy if I can't take care of him?"

Papa replied, "Dwight and Alfreda will help me raise Jimmy. We also could ask your little brother, Don, if he and Ella would take Jimmy to live with them."

The next day Papa and I had lunch together at the house. After we finished eating, he told me that Jimmy and I had to get in the car with him, because he was going to take me to the doctor.

Dr. Bartlett examined me and gave me specific tests, such as walking on the line down his hallway, touching my nose with my fingers in rapid succession, and other tests for my motor skills. He then called Papa, who was entertaining Jimmy in the waiting room. The three of us went into the doctor's office. He told us that there was actually something wrong with my motor skills, and he wanted me to go see a doctor in Kearney who specialized in neuro-dysfunctions.

Papa said to the doctor, "My main concern at this time is Jimmy's safety, and I want to know if Georgia can take care of him in her present condition."

The doctor stated, "I think it is safe for Jimmy to be under Georgia's care at this time. I do suggest that you go to Kearney within the next month to see this specialist. Or, you can bring Georgia here two months from now and I can reexamine her to see if there's any deterioration."

After dinner that evening, when Jimmy had fallen asleep on Papa's bed, Papa said, "I'll come home every afternoon for lunch to make sure things are going well with you, Georgia. On your bad days, when you can't function or when you feel out of sorts, I will ask Mrs. Huff to take Jimmy on those days. I'll also be home every evening to help feed and care for Jimmy."

I didn't like what he was saying, but after thinking about it, I agreed with him. For Jimmy's safety, we had to get extra help from somebody.

On some mornings, I would feel so tired and unable to function that Papa would take over the responsibilities for Jimmy. He would wake Jimmy, make his breakfast, feed him, and then dress him in the clothes I had laid out the prior night. Then I would get up, kiss Jimmy, and comb his hair before Papa took him to Mrs. Huff's house next door. On some days, Mrs. Huff couldn't take Jimmy. When that happened, Papa would take him to the store, and Mrs. Hess, who helped her husband run the creamery next door, would watch Jimmy for the day.

I always loved it when Jimmy came home, because I would miss him all day. He would run in the house, jump up on my lap, put his arms around my neck, and hug me as tight as he could. He placed warm kisses all over my face.

With his tiny voice, he would say, "Mama, Mama. I miss you so much."

Sometimes, I couldn't even get out of bed because I was so exhausted. I felt as if I hadn't slept all night, but I knew I did. I would keep the window shades closed during the day, because the light irritated me emotionally. I sometimes would just sit in Papa's soft leather chair and stare into space, not even thinking about anything.

On my good days, which were sporadic, the things that controlled my everyday senses were mental rather than physical events. On my good days, I could catch up with the laundry and dishes. I would get to have Jimmy on those days, and Papa would come home at noon for lunch. Jimmy was now able to walk across the room without falling down. His legs were getting chubby, and he was beginning to say two-syllable words. I loved to just sit and watch him move about and play with his wooden toys.

Papa and I went to Kearney to see the specialist. We were in his office for four hours of testing. Then he told us I had Huntington's Chorea. He said it was a hereditary disease and it runs in the women of our family. He told us that I was regressing rapidly according to the last doctor's visit in Lexington.

I cried most of the way home knowing what was in store for the remainder of my life. The doctor told Papa and I that he thought I had possibly two more months before I would become bedridden.

My conversation with Papa, as we approached Lexington, was, "Papa, my main concern at this time is what to do with little Jimmy. I love him so much."

Papa put his arm around my shoulders and drew me to him, saying, "I will take care of Jimmy until I no longer can. What I'm concerned about is my age and my health. First, we will go to our family, Dwight, Don or Thelma, to see if they will accept Jimmy into their homes. There will be no adoptions as long as I'm living. Georgia, you have been a good mother to little Jimmy, and I will make sure he will be taken care of, as long as I am alive. I, too, love him as my own."

Bill Brown aka Papa, faced another hard family decision because of the situation with his daughter and little Jimmy. He saw the signs of Huntington's Chorea affecting his daughter, and he knew he must do everything he could to protect her and Jimmy. Home care for both of them would be impossible, because he didn't have the funds. The only other option would be to commit Georgia to the state mental hospital, which was located in Hastings, Nebraska.

The next question would be what to do with Jimmy, because someone would have to take care of this one-and-one-half-year-old boy. Papa went to see Dwight who was working as a farmhand and had two children of his own at that time. Dwight couldn't get enough work during the winter months to support his family, so he had to borrow money from Papa to make it through the winter months. So, Dwight told Papa he couldn't help raise Jimmy.

Don and Ella were living in Iowa trying to sell pots and pans and were struggling to even pay their rent, let alone take on another child to feed. Ella was a very thin and nervous lady who didn't think she could handle raising another young boy. Papa couldn't make the trip to Iowa to talk to them in person, so he wrote them a letter. The letter he received in response to his request said, "Sorry, we can't take little Jimmy."

Papa called Thelma from his shop, and Frank told him they couldn't and wouldn't take Jimmy, because Frank had done enough for Georgia when she had lived with his family. Frank couldn't afford another mouth to feed. Thelma's heart was broken for she loved Georgia and Jimmy. Unfortunately, Thelma's hands were tied regarding her husband's decision. She could do nothing to make the situation right for little Jimmy's life.

Everyone in the family wondered how much longer Georgia would be able to take care of little Jimmy.

Papa wondered what he would do with Georgia when she became confined to total bedrest? What would happen to little Jimmy Brown after Georgia's physical body couldn't cope with the daily requirements to be his mother? All these questions reeled through Papa's mind, and he didn't have any answers.

Chapter 3

Living with a Disease While Raising Jimmy

On the days Georgia Brown was feeling tired and couldn't get out of bed, Jimmy would get to spend time with Uncle Dwight's children—Julie, age four, and Arlene, who was the same age as Jimmy. Jimmy loved to play with these two girls, for they were always taking care of him. On Tuesdays and Thursdays, Ruby Hess would take care of Jimmy. Her husband owned the creamery next door to Papa's shop, and she would take two days off to help with Jimmy. This schedule worked out perfectly for Papa. On special days, when Georgia wasn't feeling well or when Mrs. Hess had something personal to do, Papa would take Jimmy to the shop with him. On the mornings or afternoons when Georgia felt more energetic, she would take care of Jimmy.

"Are you feeling okay today, Georgia, so I can leave Jimmy with you?" asked Papa.

"It's a good day today, Papa. Go to work. I can take care of Jimmy," Georgia said with a lily in her voice as she smiled at her darling boy, Jimmy.

"Okay," Papa said quietly. "I'll be home for lunch." He closed the door and headed to work.

As Papa closed the door, I knew I could clean the house a little and do a load of laundry. But then I would need to lie down with Jimmy in the morning to get a little rest. While I rested, Jimmy loved to touch his little nose up against my nose and look into my eyes, with his hands cupping my cheeks. He liked to play, "Eyes-open, eyes-closed." Then we would try to see who could keep their eyes shut for the longest time. By playing that game, I would always hope that Jimmy would fall asleep.

I noticed if I kept on a regular schedule and took a nap in the morning and one in the afternoon, I could have more time with Jimmy. After supper, Jimmy and I would lie down after we both got ready for bed. Then he and I would fall asleep for the night.

I could no longer put Jimmy in the buggy and walk downtown. I didn't have enough energy to get back home, so Papa would have to buy the groceries and bring them home. I still loved to take Jimmy over to Mrs. Huff's Stop & Shop store next door.

The Brown Leather and Harness Shop was located one block north of Highway 30 in the downtown area of Lexington. At the end of the street, four huge granaries stood high above the town. The four roofs were made of red tile. We could see the granaries and their red tile roofs from miles around the flat Platte River Valley. The granary is where the local farmers brought their crops, which consisted of corn and wheat. They would sell their seeds to the granary at harvest time. The elevators would lift the corn to the top of the towers and store the corn until the rail cars arrived. Then they would fill the cars with the corn and wheat. The railroad would bring the corn and wheat into the bigger cities to sell to the flour mills and other buyers of grain.

Next door to Papa's shop was a co-op exchange; the local farmers and businessmen got together to form this organization. This is where the farmers could buy their gasoline and other products, such as seed corn that they would plant in their fields in the spring. The price of their products was at wholesale because they were buying from themselves. This is how a co-op worked.

The outside wall of Papa's shop was made of brick and was one-hundred feet long. It was located next to the co-op filling station. Alongside his shop, Papa built a couple of hitching posts for the farmers to tie their horses and wagons. The farmers would drive their wagons into town to pick up groceries and other necessities. They would tie their teams of horses to the hitching posts and bring their horses' tack into the shop for repair. Papa would estimate the repair and then tell them if he could do it right away or if the equipment would have to be left for a couple of days. They would then shop or go back over to the co-op to talk to local farmers and ranchers about what was happening and they would discuss their farming community.

In the 1940s, the farmers were converting their methods of planting and harvesting from horses to gasoline tractors. Many farmers couldn't afford to buy a tractor. A lot of the talk was that they were afraid that if they bought a tractor, the price of gasoline in the next two or three years would go up; thereby reducing their farming profit. Another concern was the cost for repairing the tractors, which they couldn't afford. Horses didn't break down and only took grain and hay to keep operating.

Papa's shop was very popular because he could repair many things for those farmers and ranchers. This would keep the farmers and ranchers going into the fields with a lot less cost than having to buy a new tractor.

Jimmy Brown got to meet those farmers and ranchers on the days when he was at the shop with Papa. Many of the farmers who came to Papa's shop had driven from the fields with their wagons and team of horses. Their repairs needed attention right away because they didn't have a second set of harnesses to continue working the fields. Some customers would have Papa repair the holes in their canvas dams that they used in irrigation ditches.

Farmers would come in during the spring and summer when the temperatures outside were hot and muggy. Many farmers didn't smell too clean. Most had old straw hats or a felt hat that had rings of sweat around the hatbands. In the summer months, some customers came in wearing their long johns with perspiration soaking the front and back, and they usually weren't wearing a shirt. Some had long, unruly hair and were unshaven, since they didn't take the time to cut their hair or shave.

Papa told me the smell would make little Jimmy wrinkle up his nose, and he would say, "PU, you stink!"

Then Jimmy would run into the workroom and stand next to Papa at the sewing machine. He would follow Papa and would sometimes hang onto his pant leg as Papa dealt with a farmer's problems. Sometimes the horses' harnesses would smell like horse sweat.

The farmers would talk to Papa and then Papa would tell them it would be twenty minutes or more before he could get the job completed. Most of the farmers would walk downtown and do their shopping and other things they needed to get done while in town. A few of the farmers would sometimes sit in the front of the shop and put Jimmy on their knee. It wasn't uncommon for them to give Jimmy a horsy ride to entertain him to occupy their time. Sometimes, Jimmy would climb off their laps and hurry over to the small saddle located in the waiting room. But he didn't like the smell, and some of the farmers scared little Jimmy.

Jimmy loved spending time with me. When I was in my bedroom sitting at the dressing table that had a big round mirror above the center of the table, he would watch me. On each side of the table were drawers where I would store my makeup. The bottom drawers were for my scarves and other items.

Jimmy loved my scarf drawer, which was a big drawer on the right side of the table. He would open it by using both hands to pull the heavy drawer open, and he'd pull out all the colorful scarves. He'd wrap the scarves around his neck and arms, which always earned a big smile from me. Then I'd tickle him and he would giggle and laugh.

One day, I was sitting on the bench in front of my mirror combing my hair. I was trying to get my hat in place when I noticed Jimmy standing next to me. Papa had dressed him in a going-to-town outfit of brown corduroy bib pants with a long-sleeved white dress shirt.

"You look very nice, Jimmy," I told him.

Then I went back to adjusting my hat with bobby pins. As quick as lightening, Jimmy slipped his hand into the blue jar of bobby pins and tipped the jar over. It crashed to the floor and all the bobby pins scattered everywhere.

I looked at Jimmy and yelled, "No. No!"

Jimmy just stood there with a sheepish look on his face.

Then I stood up and screamed, "I don't have time for this trouble."

I picked Jimmy up under the arms and carried him to the front door. I opened the door, sat him down outside on the front step, and then I closed the door. I hurried back into my room to continue getting ready for our outing.

Chapter 4

Feeling Abandoned

I knew Mama was mad that I had spilled her jar of bobby pins, but I didn't understand why she put me out here on the porch all by myself. I stood there for a while looking at the small windows way up above the doorknob. I kept waiting for my mother to look out, but she didn't even come to the door and open it. After a few minutes, I turned around and started walking down the front sidewalk, which led to the street. As I got to the street, I turned left to go to the corner, where Mama and I had gone many times to get to Huff's little grocery store, which was next door to our house. I walked past the store, and continued down to the next block and turned left again.

I began to walk and just followed the sidewalk. As I continued walking, it started to snow. I was not crying and scared; I was just walking, for I had never walked this far by myself. I was pleased with being able to walk such a distance all alone. I was only two and a half years old and was not steady on my feet. I continued to the next corner, turned left again, and walked until I came to a very busy main street.

This street had many cars driving past, so I stopped and stood there. I started to shiver and felt cold. I could feel the snowflakes on my blond hair. The big snowflakes were covering my shoulders and arms now, as I stood there and watched the snow gently falling on my outstretched arm. I pointed at the bright lights of a Conoco gas station across the street, as the sky became darker. That's when I started to cry because I couldn't get across the street.

At that same moment, the owner of the filling station was looking out the front window at the snow and he saw me standing there in my corduroy bib pants and socks with no shoes. He came running towards me, removing his blue coat as he ran. I began crying so hard that I couldn't see him coming towards me. He reached down, picked me up, and wrapped his big blue coat around me. He turned and carried me across the street to his station. I stopped crying loudly by the time we got inside and he sat me into a wooden chair next to his desk.

"Hi. I'm Mr. Crawley. I'm going to put you next to my electric heater to get you warm, and then I'm going to try to find your parents."

He removed a small heater from underneath his desk and placed it in front of the chair I was sitting in. Then he wrapped me tighter into his big blue coat.

He was speaking loudly, and said, "I'll call...oh, my God! Oh, my God! What is happening? I better call my wife. She'll know what to do."

He was frantically dialing on his black phone, which sat on his desk next to the heater. He began to talk to his wife.

"What should I do with this little frozen boy?"

There were many loud noises coming over the phone when he said, "Yes, I will," and then he hung up.

He picked me up with his strong arms, pulled a ring of keys out of his pocket, and locked the front door of the station. He took me to his car, opened the car door, and sat me in the front seat. I still had the big blue coat wrapped around me.

He started driving and then we stopped in front of a house. I was shivering and my jaws were clattering as Mr. Crowley carried me into his nice warm house. His wife had taken some warm towels out of the oven. She stood me up on the kitchen table, took off the big blue coat, and then she started taking off my soaked clothing. She had a pretty face, and was talking nice and soft to me as she hurriedly undressed me. She then gently wrapped me in those nice warm fluffy white towels. I started warming up because my legs and arms stopped shaking and my teeth stopped chattering.

Mrs. Crowley said, "Sonny, do you like hot chocolate?"

At that time, all I could do was shake my head yes.

Within minutes, she handed me a big white cup of hot chocolate to sip. She continued talking to me and remarked how much I had grown. While Mrs. Crawley was taking care of me, Mr. Crowley went across the street and knocked on the front door of Papa's house. Mr. Crowley could hear Mama walking around in the house talking to herself. Mama would not open the front door even though he kept banging his fist on the front door.

Mr. Crowley came back home and looked for Papa's phone number in the telephone book. Then he picked up the telephone, told the operator he wanted to talk to Bill Brown, and started talking to Papa. Fifteen minutes later, Papa came to the Crowley's and Mr. and Mrs. Crawley told him the whole story.

Papa went across the street and had to use his key to get inside. Mr. Crowley carried me to Papa's and that was the last time I saw Mr. Crowley.

When we got inside, Mama was sitting in the big sofa chair sound asleep.

Now Papa had another decision to make after the incident of Georgia putting Jimmy out of the house in the middle of winter. He knew he couldn't keep Jimmy safe anymore. He saw the signs of Huntington's Chorea affecting his daughter and he knew he had to do something to protect her. He didn't have sufficient funds to have someone take care of Georgia and Jimmy. The only other option would be to commit Georgia to the state mental hospital, which was located in Hastings, Nebraska.

The next question he pondered was what to do with Jimmy. He knew someone had to take care of this two-and-one-half-year-old boy, yet all his relatives refused to take Jimmy.

The next morning Papa got Jimmy up. He fed him breakfast, dressed him, and took him to Mrs. Huff's for the day. Then he came back to the house to talk to Georgia. He sat her down in his big soft chair and pulled the kitchen chair up in front of her. He sat across from her with their knees almost touching.

Papa said, "Georgia, we are now to a point where I feel that you cannot take care of Jimmy. His safety has to come first, especially after what happened yesterday. I am also concerned with your safety, because I can't afford someone to stay with you. I'm afraid you are going to have a hard time taking care of yourself. Georgia, do you agree with me?"

She shook her head yes.

Papa then leaned forward in his chair with his face in front of her face.

"Georgia, I'm going to have to look into the state hospital in Hastings to see if we can get them to take care of you." Then Papa started to explain, "I will have to take care of little Jimmy down at the shop three days a week because Dwight and Alfreda live too far out of town. I will not have enough time to take Jimmy to their house every morning before I go to work."

"I love my Jimmy," Georgia said, "but I know I can't keep him during the day. I also know you can't take care of the three of us and your shop. So I will go to the hospital, but only if you promise you will bring Jimmy as often as you can to see me."

Papa stood up and said, "Georgia, we will come to see you as often as possible, because I know you love Jimmy very much and he loves you."

From that day on, Papa took Jimmy to the shop every morning except for Tuesdays and Thursdays, when Mrs. Hess would take Jimmy home with her during the mornings when she wasn't working at the creamery.

Papa would keep Jimmy busy in the front office while he was working in the back of the shop.

Papa sold leather saddles and bridles to his customers. He had three saddles on display, which were mounted on sawhorses. Jimmy would use one of the saddles with a bridle that Papa had put together for him as his make-believe horse. Jimmy would ride the horse while the straps of the harness slapped from side to side. It provided just the right amount of entertainment for Jimmy.

Then Papa placed a sheepskin on top of one of his worktables. This woolly skin was where Jimmy would take his morning and afternoon naps. The humming of the sewing machine as Papa worked seemed to be very comforting and soothing to Jimmy as he slept on the sheepskin. Jimmy would sometimes fall asleep in the chairs in the waiting room. Sometimes Jimmy would fall asleep in the arms of a gentle farmer who would tell him a story or read him a book. Papa or another farmer would carry Jimmy into the workroom and lay him on the sheepskin.

During those times when Papa placed Jimmy on the sheepskin for his nap, Jimmy would pick at the wool and get enough of it to make a small ball of wool. He would place the ball of wool around his little curled-up index finger and then he would suck his thumb and smell the wool. The sweet smell of the sheep's wool was one of his longtime memories. This sheepskin was the place where he got his diapers changed by Papa. It also was where Jimmy had to lay down when he was naughty.

Papa called the state mental institution and spoke to someone with authority, who told him they would send him the necessary papers. He was instructed to fill out the paperwork and return it to them so they could make a final decision if they would accept Georgia.

Papa received the papers from the state. He filled them out and mailed them back.

A month later, the state hospital sent another letter to Papa, and he was requested to fill out the questionnaire about himself and his financial means. It took Papa two weeks to return it.

When Papa knew Georgia was going to have a good day, he would ask her to go with him and Jimmy down to the shop. Georgia would take care of Jimmy, and that allowed Papa to get a lot of work done. Halfway through the morning, Jimmy and Georgia would go next door to the creamery and see Mrs. Hess, or they'd visit Wally at the restaurant to get some bread pudding for Jimmy. Mrs. Hess and Georgia would sit and talk, while Mr. Hess entertained Jimmy in the back room. Mrs. Hess knew when Georgia was getting tired and she'd call for Jimmy. Then she would walk Jimmy and Georgia back to Papa's shop next door. Papa would then take them home, where Jimmy and Georgia would lie down and get their morning nap.

Three weeks later, Papa received an admissions letter from the state hospital, giving him the details of how to prepare for admission into the hospital. Papa waited for a day when he felt Georgia was coherent and in good spirits. He had taken Jimmy to see Mrs. Huff next door and had come back to talk with Georgia. Again, he put her in one of the straight-backed chairs at the dining table, and he sat straight in front of her. That's how their eye-to-eye conversation began.

Papa started by saying, "I received a letter of admission to the state hospital, and I want you to understand the procedures. We are going to pack a suitcase with the clothing you'll need. We will drive you to Hastings on November 1. They want to run some tests on you, and at the same time, you will see the facility and learn how it operates. You'll get to stay there for the first week, and then they will allow you to call me at the end of that week."

My first question was, "Papa, you and Jimmy will come to see me after that first week, right?"

Papa said, "After you make that phone call, I will speak with the administrator, and we will make a decision at that time. Yes! Jimmy and I will come to see you as often as we can."

"Will I be bedridden like Mama was within the next six months?"

"Georgia," Papa said, "we don't know what kind of condition you will be in at that time until we see the test results, which will help us make a decision."

"Will I get to see you and Jimmy every two weeks?"

At that moment, Papa stood up still holding onto her hands and said, "Jimmy and I will come to see you whenever we can get away from the shop."

Papa stared intently into her eyes, and asked, "Do you understand our conversation, Georgia?"

She said, "I understand what is about to happen on the first of November. However, I still want to know if you will come to see me at least every month."

Without answering, Papa placed me in his big soft chair with a wooden chair in front of me. Then he went next door, picked up Jimmy, and the two of them went to his shop.

That morning I sat in the big soft chair, and I began to wonder what would happen to Jimmy if I stayed in the hospital. I climbed up on the wooden chair and scooted myself backwards to the bed in my bedroom. I climbed up on the bed, tried to go to sleep for my nap, but I was more concerned with what was going to happen to Jimmy.

Papa and Jimmy came home for lunch and Papa made some grilled cheese sandwiches, which Jimmy loved. Jimmy climbed up on my lap and gave me a big hug. Then he grabbed my cheeks as he kissed me above each eye.

He looked me straight in the eyes with his beautiful blue eyes and said, "Mama, I love you."

Then he turned and started eating his lunch. During the meal, Jimmy was telling me in his three-word sentences, about all the people and things he shot while riding his horse at the shop. I turned my chair towards Papa and asked him to turn towards me.

I asked Papa, "What will happen to Jimmy if I go to the hospital?"

Papa looked me directly in the eyes, waited for a few moments, and then said, "I will take care of Jimmy until he reaches school age. Then I will put him in a boarding school so he will have the proper guidance and education. I will not allow him to be adopted, because I love him as much as my own. I am too old and do not have the energy to take care of Jimmy when he will be ready for school."

Then he asked me a question, "Georgia, do you approve of this plan? I cannot think of any other way to protect Jimmy. None of your brothers or sisters can see it in their hearts to take little Jimmy. So I will take him, for I love him, as I know you love him."

The day came for Papa to take Georgia to the state hospital in Hastings. Papa drove out to Dwight and Alfreda's little rented house to pick them up for the trip. Dwight sat up front while Papa drove his old 1934 Ford sedan. Alfreda and Georgia had Jimmy in between them in the back seat. The ride to Hastings took two-and-one-half hours. Alfreda brought sandwiches and coffee to help ease the trip.

Everyone got very quiet as we drove onto the hospital's grounds. We had never seen such a sight. There were tall trees and many big, white buildings with a lot of landscaping around the buildings. It was winter and everything looked bleak with no leaves on the trees. We didn't see anyone outside those big three-story white buildings. As we drove into the driveway, Papa told Mama that Jimmy would stay in the car with Alfreda, and he and Dwight would go into the hospital to check Mama in at the front desk.

After hearing those words, tears rolled down Mama's cheeks. She hugged Jimmy to the point where it looked like he could barely breathe.

All Jimmy could say was, "Mama, you hurt me!"

Then Alfreda reached over and squeezed Mama's arm with her big hand. Mama let go and started kissing me all over my face again.

As the car came to a halt, Papa told Dwight to get Mama's suitcase out of the trunk and bring it in with us. Papa walked to Mama's side of the car and opened her door. He took Mama by her arm to help her out of the car. Mama resisted his grasp. Then Papa leaned over close to her ear.

He whispered, "It's time to go and to let Jimmy loose."

Mama kissed Jimmy for the longest time and then looked deep in his eyes.

She said," Jimmy, you are my love and I will love you forever!" Then she whispered something in his ear.

At that moment, she let go of him, and with Papa's help, she slipped into her raccoon coat that she loved, and got out of the car. The three of them walked towards the big white building. As they got to the first of many steps, Mama turned and looked back at the car, with tears in her eyes. She blew jimmy a big kiss from her dark gloved hand.

Alfreda watched from inside the car and saw tears rolling down Jimmy's cheeks.

"I'm not supposed to cry," Jimmy told Alfreda.

Alfreda wrapped Jimmy in her hug.

He looked up at her and said, "Mama whispered in my ear, 'Be a big boy. Don't cry for Mama when I leave you today.'"

That was the last time he ever saw her alive. Her funeral was sixteen years later.

Chapter 5

Life without Mama

It was a heartbreaking day when Papa had to commit his daughter, Georgia, into the care of those at the mental institution. The fast progression of Huntington's Chorea disease was unexpected, but in his deepest thoughts, he knew she would be safe and taken care of.

On the ride back home, Papa asked Dwight and Alfreda if they could take care of Jimmy for a couple weeks. Papa explained that it would be a positive transition for Jimmy after losing his mother because he could play with their daughters. The distraction would keep him busy, and then Papa would have a chance to make arrangements for Jimmy's care.

"Of course," Alfreda said with a smile. We'd love to have Jimmy stay with us on the farm for a couple weeks, right Dwight?"

"Yes," Dwight answered, looking in the rearview mirror at Jimmy. "Jimmy, you're going to the farm with us for a couple weeks. We'll have fun."

Jimmy smiled, and said, "Papa, are you coming to the farm with us too?"

Papa turned around and looked at Jimmy sitting in the back seat with Alfreda. "I have to work at the harness shop, Jimmy, but I'll come to visit every weekend. How does that sound?"

I spent two weeks on the farm with Dwight, Alfreda, and their two daughters, Julie and Arlene. I don't remember missing Mama as much as I would have if I had gone home with Papa. He came to visit me on the weekends, and I started missing him when he wasn't there. At the end of the two weeks, he brought me home and every day I would go with him to the shop. We usually ate lunch downtown at Wally's Café, and that kept my mind off Mama.

Wally Haggard, the owner of the café, would join us for lunch and we would laugh a lot. When Papa and I got home in the evening, I would run from room to room looking for Mama, but she was not in the house. I would start to cry and then Papa would pick me up and sit with me in his big, soft, leather chair. He consoled me with his gentle, quiet voice, and he held me close to him. Papa hugged me a lot in those first few months.

Mrs. Hess told Papa she could no longer take care of me on Tuesdays and Thursdays, because her husband's business was growing and he needed her help in the office. Papa was trying to run his business and take care of me—a two-year-old boy—at the same time. This certainly was a chore for him. He would dress me, change my diapers, put me down for a nap, and entertain me. He did all these things while trying to conduct his business. That was a lot to ask of a seventy-two-year-old man.

Papa was a small man with thinning silver hair, and he wore silver, round glasses that hooked behind his ears. I loved to sit in the bathroom and watch him shave all the white cream off his face with a straight razor. Sometimes as he lathered his face, he would turn towards me. With his fingers, he would touch my nose with the lather to make me laugh.

Outdoors, he always wore a gray felt hat with sweat stains just above a small linen band around the crown of the hat.

During summer, he wore his yellow straw, fine woven hat, which had a wide blue band around the base of the crown. When he worked in the shop, he put his hat on the hat rack in the front waiting room. He wore long-sleeved white shirts with a thin rubber armband to keep his right forearm sleeve tight. Did I ever know why? I guess he did it was out of habit; maybe it was to keep his sleeves out of his sewing machine while he worked on the heavy leather products. He lost his right index finger at the knuckle joint while he was using the sewing machine. This happened before I lived with him.

He wore baggy dress pants with slim black suspenders and he always wore long johns. He bathed maybe twice a week but he did his own laundry without bleach once every two weeks; his underwear was not too white. He didn't iron any of his shirts after Mama left us.

I spent a lot of time with Papa in his workshop, and to this day, I remember the many smells that were associated with his harness and bridle business. A display room was the first thing I saw when walking through the front door. It served as a waiting area for farmers and ranchers who needed their leather and harness goods right away. They could sit in the wooden, high-back chairs with accompanying three-legged stools. One of the walls contained floor-to-ceiling shelves that held saddles, harnesses, and other leather goods that Papa had repaired.

I don't remember seeing dust on any of the shelves or chairs, due to the frequent use. The only thing that needed cleaning was the floor. It had to be swept often. Papa would sweep his workshop when all the dirt fell off the canvas dams or the pieces of material that were piled up on the floor. This was a man's place, and the only time women were present was when Mama would come for lunch.

There were two windows on either side of the front door. On the front windows that faced the street, you could read the inscribed lettering, "Brown's Leather and Harness Shop." In the front waiting room, there were usually two or three sawhorses with new saddles astride them. Always hanging in the front windows were two or three new bridles, along with three horse collars to show to the public. These were the newest bridles for different needs of the farmers.

You had to walk through swinging half-doors in the waiting room to get into the workroom that was three times longer than the waiting room. The only light shining into the workroom came through the skylight windows high on the back wall. There were no windows or doors on the east wall of the building—the side that was next to the co-op station.

Three huge 10' x 10' wooden worktables were located on the left side of the workroom. Those tables were so large they could hold huge rolls of cowhide or canvas on them for cutting and repairing tears and holes in the canvases. The farmers who irrigated their fields used those canvases as water dikes. They would put them at the end of the irrigation ditches to direct the water to where the farmer needed it to reach the plants that were growing in the fields.

On the right side of the room closest to the stove was Papa's special heavy-duty sewing machine. He used that one for making and repairing large pieces of canvas and awnings. He also had a sewing machine to repair lighter materials, such as horse blankets and harnesses.

Against the back wall, next to the sewing machines, was an L-shaped bench with four rather large holes in the top of the bench. Each hole held big brown glass jars of different types of glue. Papa used glue to adhere cloth and leather together before he would sew them. The big jar of rubber cement glue was the most-used jar, and it had a big paintbrush that Papa used on most of his leather repairs. One of the other smells from the table included turpentine, which Papa would brush on the leather to make it soft and pliable.

During those times when I played around the worktable and Papa was gluing, he would tell me, "Jimmy, put your hand out on this table."

I would stand on my tiptoes and put my hand up on the leather that he was working on. He then would take the brush with the glue and swipe it across the top of my hand.

Then he would say, "Turn your hand over, Jimmy."

I would turn my hand over and he would swipe the brush across the palm of my hand.

Then he would say, "Put your hand up in the air until I tell you to put it down."

The rubber glue would dry on my hand.

After awhile, he would then say, "Jimmy, now you can pull the glue off your hand."

Pulling the glue off my hand took me a long time. I think he did this to keep me busy from interrupting him while he finished his work.

Close to the back door of the workroom was a small coal bin. Coal was used to start a fire in the potbelly stove during the winter to keep the two rooms warm. When it was cold outside, we would wear our coats for one or two hours in the morning until the room got warm.

I rode my make-believe horse most days while at Papa's shop. As I got older, I wanted to do more interesting things, especially if no farmers or ranchers were in the waiting room to entertain me. Some mornings, I would wait until I heard Papa's sewing machine making the whirling noise, which meant he was busy. I would climb down off the make-believe horse, open the front door and wander out on the front sidewalk. I would look for sticks, paper, and little rocks to play with. A couple of times Papa looked for me outside on the sidewalk when he didn't hear me making noise in the waiting room. Soon after, he placed a cowbell above the door so it would ring when anybody opened the front door. Sometimes Papa was too busy concentrating on his sewing, and he didn't hear the bell when I went exploring outside.

During warm weather, I would go down the street wearing only my little white cotton undershirt and droopy diaper. Papa was not one to change my diapers very often, since he had deadlines to meet with his repairs. If Mrs. Hess who worked next door at the creamery was looking out her front window and saw me, she would pick me up and bring me into her shop or take me back to Papa.

Sometimes without anyone noticing, I would go next door to Niemi's Shoe Shop. The doorknob was too high for me to reach even if I got up on my tiptoes, so then I would go around the corner to the paint store's front door.

After escaping from Papa's shop two or three times, I learned that if I waited outside of those doors, someone would eventually come out of the store. I could quickly grab the door before it shut and I could get inside the store. The owner or workers in the store would stop and make a fuss over me. Then they would call Papa, because he had left his number at all the businesses on that street after the first time I went exploring.

Mrs. Hess had a sister named Mabel who lived around the corner on Washington Street. She had an apartment above the businesses on Main Street in Lexington. Mrs. Hess had arranged for her sister to take care of me in the afternoons. Mabel would come to Papa's around noon. Together, Mabel and I would walk to her apartment as I pulled my wooden toy train behind me. I would have lunch, and then hopefully, a nap. We would play with some of her toys, and then she would place a blanket on the front room floor with a fan moving back and forth to keep her apartment as cool as possible.

I would fall asleep as soon as I could pick some of the blanket fuzz off and make a little ball of wool. She would let me sleep as long as I wanted, but at first, I would wake up and not know where I was. That's when I started crying real loud. Mabel had a hard time quieting me down. She got upset and told Papa she couldn't take care of me because I was crying every afternoon. The only time after my nap when I wasn't crying was when she picked me up and carried me back to Papa's shop. He would then take me into the workshop, and lie me on the sheepskin table with my blanket.

Some evenings after Papa finished working, we would go to different places, such as the Odd Fellows Hall, where he was a member. He would clean me up, feed me, and then we'd go back downtown. He picked me up and climbed many stairs to get to the Odd Fellows Hall above the Rialto Theatre. I always had my wooden toy train to play with while he was in his meetings. After the meeting, and every Tuesday evening, four or five men would gather upstairs and play pinochle until approximately eleven o'clock.

Papa always had a chair next to him while he played cards. I would play with my wooden toy train, and when I started to get sleepy, Papa would put me in the chair next to him. I would curl up in the chair, watching the cigarette smoke curl around the faces and heads of the men playing cards. Then I would drift off to sleep. Later, Papa would carry me down to his car and we would go home.

Some evenings, we would go over to the Hess's for they loved to play pinochle card games with Papa and their next door neighbors. Papa and I would go over to the Hess's early for dinner, and I would get a bath and my diaper changed. Then Mrs. Hess would put me into my nice warm pajamas. I would get to lie on the couch and fall asleep until they were finished playing cards. Again, Papa would take me home and I would always end up in his big featherbed sleeping with him.

Papa always did the laundry on Saturdays, so I had to be out on the back porch with him. On most Saturday mornings, the sun would come in through the windows on the back porch. The sunlight fell on the floor next to the kitchen door. I loved sitting in the warm sunshine on the floor playing with my wooden train. I noticed little fuzzy dust particles flying in the sunlight. Those dust particles didn't fly around outside of the sun's rays coming in through the windows. I would stand up in the sunshine, trying to catch those fuzzy dust particles.

One day, trying to catch the dust particles, I fell and landed on my backside. All of a sudden, thousands of flying dust particles appeared. I giggled and thought I could catch more of those little fuzzy things. So I began standing up and flopping down on the seat of my pants, laughing out loud. Papa saw what I was doing, and he started laughing, too. We both watched the dust particles in the sun's rays coming through the window.

Papa loved it when he and I would do things together, such as make cinnamon toast, like my mama used to make for me some mornings.

Papa would sit me on the kitchen counter, and let me spread the butter on the bread, after he had everything in place. He would carefully put the sugar spoon in my hand after he had loaded it with sugar. Then he would help me, with the guidance of his hand, and we would sprinkle sugar on top of the butter. Finally, we would take the cinnamon shaker and sprinkle the cinnamon on top of the sugar. He then would put the cinnamon bread in the lower broiler and let it melt into the bread until it became toasted.

On another occasion, Papa brought me a little three-month-old black puppy from one of his friends. He wanted me to have a companion to play with when I got home in the evenings. This puppy and I became good friends, and I started calling him Nicky. He was a black terrier with a very smooth coat of black hair. Nicky had a quarter-sized white spot of hair between his eyes and another white spot the size of my little hand on his chest. Other than that, he was coal black. He had pointed ears, and when he and I would play, he had a tail that wouldn't quit wagging.

A three-man committee made an appointment to meet with Papa at his shop in regards to Jimmy. Apparently the townsfolk had major concerns about his well-being and about their ability to concentrate on business during the day with a young child roaming the streets downtown unsupervised.

They suggested Papa could hire an all-day babysitter. Papa told them he didn't have the funds to pay for a full-time babysitter. The second suggestion was adoption—someone from the community or perhaps a relative could take care of Jimmy during the day.

Papa said he had no relatives who wanted to take me at that time. He also mentioned he didn't want me to be placed for adoption, because he loved me too much.

The three businessmen told Papa he must make a decision about what to do with me, and they would give him two weeks to find a solution.

One of the businessmen, a banker, shook Papa's hand, and told him there was an orphanage for children located in Holdrege, a town about thirty-five miles from Lexington. The man told Papa that last month he had attended one of their fundraising functions, and maybe he could consider that as an option.

Chapter 6

The Car Ride That Changed Jimmy's Life

After weighing all his options for how to best provide for Jimmy, Papa made an appointment with the admissions department of the orphanage located in Holdrege, Nebraska, thirty-five miles southeast of Lexington. Papa wanted to see if the orphanage was suitable to handle Jimmy's care, if they had the capacity to take him in, and he also wanted to inquire about the costs.

Little Jimmy Brown, at age three, was taking his first long road trip in Papa's dark green model T Ford. The inside had black leather upholstery, and the jumper seat in the back contained all of Jimmy's clothing that was stuffed into a brown cloth satchel.

"Where are we going, Papa?" Jimmy asked.

"To an orphanage," Papa stated without much expression on his face.

"What's an orphanage?" Jimmy asked.

"You'll see when we get there," Papa said.

I shifted my weight and sat with my two legs under my bottom so I could see out the window. I saw many green fields and some cows. Before too long, we drove up a long road and Papa parked in front of a big red brick building.

Papa gently picked me up out of the seat, and the next thing I knew, my little white leather shoes were touching the ground. I was dressed in a white, somewhat-ironed shirt and blue halter shorts. I took Papa's big hand and together we walked toward the huge building in front of us.

Papa and I walked to the front part of the building hand-in-hand, where there were many steps leading up to a large porch that had a big white front door. Papa and I started climbing the steps one at a time. About halfway up, I got tired of climbing and Papa had to stop. He bent over to pick me up and carried me to the big white door. Papa opened the door and stepped into a wide hallway. There was a big opening to the right of the hallway like a window, where a lady was sitting. She was typing with a lot of clacking noises coming out of the typewriter. As she typed and looked up, she saw Papa and I approaching her window.

She smiled and said, "You two must be the Browns. Would you mind stepping into the parlor across the hall and have a seat? I'll get the superintendent."

The parlor had two, black, leather, wingback chairs. On one wall, there was a small stuffed couch covered with big flower patterned material. Two, tall, wall lamps stood in each corner of the small room. I saw a picture of a man with outstretched arms and he had something shining around his head. This man had long hair and a beard on his face, but I couldn't figure out why he was not wearing shoes in the picture.

A big tall man wearing a brown suit, white shirt, and a patterned tie walked toward us. He shook Papa's hand and then he patted me on the head. I grabbed onto Papa's sleeve and slid closer to him. The man started telling Papa the rules for young children in the home. He explained that with me living in this Christian environment, I would benefit by his caring staff.

Soon a teenage girl dressed in a white shirt and blue corduroy skirt with tie-up black shoes, came into the parlor. She sat beside me on the couch. She noticed that I was still hanging onto Papa's sleeve. She waited for awhile and kept looking at me. Then she started making her fingers move funny in front of her face. She started making funny faces with her ears and nose, all while staring at me. She had long blonde hair and deep green eyes with a wide smile. I just looked at this person doing her gyrations with her fingers.

After a few minutes of watching her, I smiled, but I didn't laugh. Then she started talking to me. I kept my head down for I didn't know what she wanted. I answered all her questions with a nod or else I shook my head. By this time, I wasn't hanging onto Papa's sleeve. I was sitting on the couch, and she was kneeling on the floor in front of me.

She left the room and came back with a small teddy bear and handed it to me. She told me the bear was her friend and he wanted to play with me. She started making the bear talk to me and she made happy sounds. The superintendent and Papa were still talking, but after a while, the superintendent turned to the young girl and told her to take me down to the playroom to play with the other children.

By this time, I was talking to her and her bear. I felt like I had found a friend. She asked Papa if she could take me to the playroom to show me off to the other girls. Papa was sitting in one of the wing-backed chairs, and he said it would be perfectly all right for her to take me. She took me by my hand and we went down the hall until we reached a staircase. She led me downstairs to the next floor. I could smell cooking aromas coming up the staircase as we walked down the shiny hallway. She was talking to me all the while. She told me we were going to find her friends and they would really love to see me.

As we approached the stairs, the girl bent down and scooped me up to her waist. I held onto her with my arms wrapped around her neck, and I hugged her. With my other hand, I carried the teddy bear and held onto it tightly. We descended the stairs. I could smell her sweet clean hair, which reminded me of Mama. It had been more than two years since my mama had gone to the big white building that was surrounded with many tall trees.

I could hear a lot of laughter and screaming as we approached the playroom. I drew back and buried my face into her blonde hair.

She slowed down and said, "Don't be afraid. These girls are my friends, and I will watch out for you."

When we turned the corner, we entered this big room filled with many different size girls. I had never seen so many girls in one spot. Some were playing with a ball. Some were coloring in books, and there were many girls skipping rope.

The tall blonde girl who was holding me announced with a show-off attitude, "This is Jimmy Brown, and he is coming here to play with us today."

All the girls gathered around and started talking to me. I felt like I was going to cry. I was scared of all these girls.

"Girls, give Jimmy some space. He's not used to us."

The girls started backing off, but four girls started reaching out, as they wanted to hold me. I resisted for a while until the girl holding me looked me in my eyes.

She said, "Jimmy, these are my best friends, and I want you to hug their necks."

I turned to the tall, brown-haired girl and squeezed her neck as she took me from the blonde girl. After that, the girls passed me around and took turns holding me. I liked the attention, and I liked the smell of several girls' hair. I smiled and laughed as the girls hugged me and whirled me around to get me to laugh. I had never seen so many girls, nor gotten so much attention. Maybe an orphanage was where I wanted to be.

A bell rang and each girl headed into a different direction, except for the dark-haired girl who was still holding me. She said something about dinnertime. The blonde girl who had taken me to the playroom—her name was Ginger—came over and took me from the girl who was holding me. Ginger took me outside to show me off to the boys.

Once outside, I noticed that it was getting dark and I started looking for Papa to come get me for supper.

My first words were, "I want my Papa."

Ginger was talking to an older boy and didn't really hear me. I began to cry and started looking around to see if I could see Papa. The blond-haired, dimple-chin boy suggested that Ginger should take me back to the parlor to find my Papa.

I stopped crying as the three of us walked up the back stairs, which led into the big house. We got to the parlor on the second floor. This was where Papa and the big man had been sitting and talking when I left with Ginger. The boy and Ginger didn't find anyone except the lady behind the desk. She was now turning out lights and closing her window for the day.

She came over to Ginger, who was holding me. The lady told the boy to come in the office. Then she whispered something to him, and he, in turn, talked softly in Ginger's ear. Then Ginger tightened her arms around me as we began walking down the hall to the dining room. I began sensing that something wasn't right. I started crying for my Papa because she was walking in the wrong direction, and away from the front door.

Entering the dining hall, I was shouting, "Papa, Papa."

I was crying at the top of my lungs. Some of the girls came over and tried to stop me from crying. One of them brought my teddy bear over to see if I would take it. I was so upset that I pushed Teddy away and kept on crying.

I pointed to the stairs crying, "Papa, Papa."

The girls told Ginger to take me upstairs to find Papa. As she started going upstairs, suddenly I stopped crying. We were going to find my Papa. Ginger took me back to the parlor, talking all the while about how Papa would be somewhere. Papa was not in the parlor when we got there, so I pointed to the superintendent's office. Ginger went to the door and turned the knob. It was locked. I was getting ready to cry.

She told me we would go out front to see if Papa was in the car. Outside, Ginger and I stood on the top steps of the front porch. Papa's car was not parked in front of the home. I started to cry again, and the girl took me upstairs to the crib room. I couldn't stop crying because I felt that Papa was lost forever.

The crib room had ten to twelve cribs, which were raised high off the ground. All the vertical bars were made out of brown metal and they made a lot of noise when the sides were let down or when the children moved inside. It was like a rattling sound. The crib room was next to the girls' sleeping room, so the girls could take care of the babies when there were problems in the middle of the night. Ginger sat in a chair and started rocking and shushing me when we got into the room. There were three to four rocking chairs for this purpose.

My loud cries had stopped, and now I was only whimpering and taking deep breaths. My soft gasping sounds were slowly diminishing as my eyes were closing. I was so tired from crying. As soon as Ginger laid me down in the crib, I was suddenly startled. I sat straight up as soon as she pulled the metal sides up to the top with a loud clanking sound. I stood up and starting shaking the crib by holding onto the metal bars. I rattled the crib more, which made a loud rumbling noise. Ginger rushed over to pick me up. Then she placed me over her shoulder. She picked up a blue wool blanket and draped it over my head to keep me quiet. I liked this position, being over her shoulder. I could feel the warmth of her body, as this was what my mama used to do with me when she put me to sleep.

She started rocking me again in the rocking chair. I grabbed the blanket and began picking at the wool, finding enough to make a ball of wool. I then placed the ball of wool in my curled up right forefinger. With this, I placed my thumb in my mouth, while sniffing the wool. I fell asleep just as I had done when napping on the sheepskin wool at Papa's shop. Ginger waited a long time before she dared to put me back in the crib. Only when I was sound asleep did she lay me down in the crib. Pulling the side rail up very gently, she snapped it into the locked position.

Two hours later, I woke up and was scared to be alone in the dark. I missed Papa who would always sleep next to me. All I could see as I stood up in the crib were white sheets or something draped over something next to where I was standing. I let out a little whining noise to get Papa's attention. I wondered when Papa would come to pick me up and cuddle with me. But Papa never came, so I started crying a soft cry and waited for him to come to comfort me.

As my eyes got used to the dark, I noticed that I was in a metal cage, and I saw other metal cages all around me. Many of them had white sheets draped over the top of them, but still, I didn't see Papa. I grabbed the bars, which were cold to my hands, and I started shaking the bars back and forth. They made a lot of rattling noise that echoed off the walls of the small room where all the cribs were located. I didn't know what those metal cages were, because I was used to sleeping with Papa on his featherbed, and before that I slept with Mama.

The children in cages next to mine began making noise. Then some girls from the dormitory rushed into the crib room to see what was causing the disturbance. One of the girls had turned on the overhead lights, which were very bright to my eyes. I began seeing other cribs moving and then I heard other children starting to cry.

Someone pulled me out of my crib and held me tightly in her arms. She carried me to the rocking chair and started rocking me, while the other girls in the room were making shushing noises to the other kids who were beginning to wake up. The girls would place the other kids on their stomachs and gently shake them back and forth to get them to go back to sleep. Otherwise, they would just place their hands on the middle of the babies' backs as they lay on their stomachs.

The girl who was holding me again put a wool blanket over my head. When I started picking the wool ball again, I fell asleep with my forefinger holding the wool and sucking my thumb. The best part about this was having a warm body against my stomach, like my mama used to do to me before I went to sleep at night. This was heaven, where I came from two years ago.

The morning arrived and I could see soft lights on the ceiling as the sun came through the window shade. Within minutes, the whole room filled with a bright reddish orange light from the sun reflecting through the shade. The rattling of the cribs started very softly as the tiny bodies started to wake up and made small sucking and grunting noises. Faint crying began, but the girls started coming in to pull the sheets off the top of the cribs. They let down the sides of the cribs and picked up little children to comfort them.

The crib next to me had a small-socked foot that came out from under the sheet. It stuck out of the crib slots with wiggly toes moving in the air. Then an arm started pulling on the sheet that was on top of the crib. The sheet dropped to the floor and there was another small person lying on his back with his head turned and looking at me.

During the next four days, my main function was trying to find Papa. A few girls living in this huge building carried me wherever I wanted because I couldn't find Papa.

I felt sad and would cry a lot. First Mama left me, and then Papa left me. And I thought, *Is this what Papa meant when he said we were going to an orphanage? Is this the orphanage?*

Every morning for a week at a time, assignments were given to the girls whose job it was to take care of us kids. After getting us out of our cribs, they would then undress us, and carry us into the girl's dormitory to a small room where there were two small bathtubs. The girls would then give us a bath, diaper us, and dress us for the day. Then they'd take us to the elevator, and we would go down to the dining room for breakfast. The dining room was on the bottom floor on the east side of the building.

The dining hall had about forty long tables with benches that seated five boys or girls on each side of the table. Girls sat on the east side of the room, and the boys sat on the west side of the room. Each person had an assigned seat, which corresponded to their sleeping rooms—East Room, West Room, or Big West room. The crib-room babies, like me, had their own high-chair section, which was located in the girls' section. The assigned girls would help the matron feed the crib kids during each meal.

At the front of the dining room was a long table with a white tablecloth. It held fine dining-ware and had cushioned dining chairs for the staff to sit in and eat. The kitchen was located at the back of the dining room and had a high counter, which divided the two rooms. As we finished our meals, we carried all our own dirty dishes to the designated areas on the counter.

After breakfast, the girls would take us to a small room on the bottom floor, and they would dress us in warm clothing and take us out to the sandbox to play. Sometimes they would give us rides on the merry-go-round or put us on the teeter-totters. They were responsible for changing our diapers and taking us to the preschool room. One of the staff members, who was the instructor, would oversee us while we played games or participated in small art projects.

Halfway through the morning, we would have to get our little blankets and lie down to take a nap. Following our nap was snack time and playroom time again. Then they would change our diapers before taking us back to the dining hall for lunch with all the boys and girls. There were about ten of us children, ages three and four in the crib-room group. The afternoons consisted of playroom, nap, and again, outside playtime. Of course, this only occurred after a lot of diaper changing, nose blowing, and stop-crying techniques that were applied for various reasons.

The first two weeks after Papa left me were very hard for me, as well as all the girls who were in charge of me. I threw temper tantrums and cried most of the time, especially if they left me alone. At nap times, I would try to bite the other little children as they lay close to me on their little blankets. What I wanted was to have somebody hold me, and I wanted to wrap my arms around the girls' necks. I wanted to wrap my feet around their waists and bury my head in their hair. That was my comfort zone.

I began to realize that this life was not going to change. I slowly got accustomed to the living pattern of the crib-room kids, as we were called by everyone in the orphanage.

I was in the crib room until I was five years old, and then the girls' matron, Alice, walked me across the third-floor staircase to the boys' dormitory. She carried all the clothing I had been given, and then she introduced me to the boys' matron, Betty. She took me to the Boys East Room. She showed me my bed and my locker—number eighteen—where I was to keep everything in a specific order. Betty told me some rules to follow and introduced me to Jerry, whose bed was next to mine. I was instructed to follow him for the next couple of days to learn the routine used by the boys in this room, such as bed bells, change of clothing, and chapel time.

This was like graduation, because girls were no longer attending to me, and I was told to act like a big boy. I had to follow the lead of the other boys in the East Room. The boys' dormitory rooms were on the third floor across from the staircase, and across the main hallway from the girls' dormitories.

The East Room consisted of little boys from five years old to seven years old. The West Room was for boys who were eight to thirteen years old. Big West was for the fourteen-to seventeen-year-olds. Then there was a small room located off the staircase section next to the enclosed patio porch. It was just above the parlor room on the second floor. In this room were five or six beds for the older guys who were high school seniors or home boys who worked at the orphanage until they were drafted into the service. Some of them stayed there while trying to obtain a job before they went on their own way.

When entering the boys' dormitory, the East Room was the first room on the left, which had twenty beds in that long room. The south wall had six to eight large outside windows covered with see-through curtains and pull-down window shades. Ten beds, all with matching bedspreads were under the windows. The other ten beds were placed on the opposite side of the room with the same matching bedspreads. The beds were separated by three long benches down the middle of the room. At each end of the room were tall, green lockers. Each boy had his own locker.

Now that I was in the East Room, I learned how to dress myself and brush my teeth in the sink room, which was across the hall in the bathroom. The bathroom had twenty sinks with twenty different toothbrushes lined up with our names on the brushes as well as on the wall. The brushes belonged to the East Room boys, where the other room boys kept their toothbrushes, tooth powder, and their lockers. This bathroom was used by each group of boys. When it was time for them to get up and get ready for the day, tooth powder was placed next to each sink. I would shake the toothpaste powder can into my hand. Then I'd put my toothbrush under the running water, and dip the brush in the powder in my hand. This is how I would brush my teeth and rinse my mouth out every morning before breakfast. I'd do the same thing every evening before going to bed. While growing up during this time, there wasn't toothpaste, as we know it today.

The room next to the sink room was where the showers were located. They had white tiled walls, and there were ten showers along one wall. On the other side of the shower room was a big white bathtub where all the little kids stood in line outside the shower room door on bath day. Three East Room boys at a time would climb into the bathtub and the matron would then bathe each boy. The little guys got a bath every other day because of their dirty bodies and hands. When the matron inspected us every evening before we got undressed, she would sometimes have to change the bath water after the sixth or eighth boy, because the water was so black with dirt. Showers for the older boys were scheduled for every Tuesday and Friday before they got into bed for the night.

On the second floor, which had a shiny black tiled hall, were twelve to fifteen doors on either side of the hallway. This is where the working staff had their rooms. They lived at the home while they worked there. At the end of this long hall was the library. We could read books that had been given to the home by the local people.

Papa had left me at the orphanage during May of 1943, when I was three years old. Two years later, at Easter, Papa drove to the orphanage in his new car. The matron, Betty, sent Hank Pool outside to get me and bring me upstairs. She had packed a small paper bag with some of my clothing. Once I got upstairs, Betty told me there was someone to see me downstairs. She brought me to the parlor on the second floor, and there stood Papa in his long black overcoat and a black felt hat. I looked at him and didn't really know him, because I had not seen him for a long time. I turned towards Betty who was holding my little bag of clothing and I moved real close to her.

Papa told Betty to sit next to me until he and I got to know each other again. I sat on the couch with my arms crossed and my lips closed very tight. I didn't really know if this person was the same man who had left me without saying good-bye.

Papa removed his hat and I saw his fine, white hair. Then he reached into his coat pocket and pulled out my wooden toy train and said, "Jimmy, you left this at my house, and I wanted to bring it to you. I know you've missed it very much."

He began to hand it to me, but when he saw I wasn't reaching for the train, he placed it on the floor in front of me. When he put it there, I kicked it up in the air with my foot. I didn't say anything to him, because he had hurt me deeply in my heart.

Papa said, "Jimmy, I am sorry that I left you here, but I had to, for reasons I will explain to you someday. Forgive me and let's be friends again."

He picked up my little bag of clothing and reached out for my hand. I looked at his big hand, and I looked into his eyes. His eyes were gentle and kind as they always had been. I put my hand in his big hand and slid off the couch. I picked up the string that was attached to my little wooden train and I pulled the train as we walked towards the front door. I turned and waved to Betty.

I still didn't say anything as Papa opened the door to his new green car. He placed me on a big soft cushion that he had put there on the front seat so I could look out the window as he drove. We drove back to Lexington, and I didn't say anything to Papa. I only listened.

He talked to me about Mrs. Hess, and told me how she missed me. He said she wanted the two of us to come over for dinner one night this week. He also talked about Nicky, my dog, who would be excited about me coming home. He said he had sold his shop and retired, and with the money he had saved, he bought this new car for himself. I would be able to spend a whole week at Papa's before I would have to return to the children's home.

I didn't say anything to Papa, because I was still confused about why he had left me at the home, and now all of a sudden here he was taking me back to his house. I got out of the car and opened the front door to Papa's house. As soon as I got inside, Nicky came running towards me. He jumped up on my chest with his front paws and knocked me down. Nicky then began licking my face, and I broke out in laughter. I squirmed on the floor because he was pushing at my body and jumping on me. Then he grabbed hold of my pant's leg and started shaking my leg back and forth, which made me squeal with laughter. I started liking Papa again.

I hollered, "Papa, Papa, please help me!"

With a lot of laughter and squealing from me, Papa reached down and touched Nicky on his head. Nicky stopped, looked up at Papa, and began running through the house. He ran out the front door of the house and around the house to the back door. He opened the screen door with his nose as he ran through the door. By this time, I was up on my feet and Nicky grabbed my pant's leg again. He started shaking my leg back and forth until I fell down again, laughing and squealing. Finally, I grabbed Nicky with both hands. Only then, did he settle down and let me pet him and hug him. We were pals forever.

Papa and I became friends again. We did all the fun things we used to do—made cinnamon toast in the broiler, popped popcorn in the iron skillet, and he let me help him make the pancake batter. Almost every day that we were together, he told me he would be taking me back to the home at the end of the week. However, he said he would come back to get me in a couple of months so I could spend the summer with him.

I didn't know if Papa was telling the truth, but for now, I believed him.

Chapter 7

Orphanage Rules Helped Shape Jimmy's Young Life

My life at the orphanage revolved around getting to know the routines, the rules, and who was in charge. Plus, with eighty boys and girls living at the home, there was always lots going on and plenty of chores for all of us.

I was in contact every morning and evening with the matron of the boys' dormitory. During the nine years I lived at the orphanage, there were six matrons who took care of me. Most of them would live at the orphanage for three or four years and they were all especially nice to us kids. While each of us were learning how to do life in the home, a matron had to work six days a week and fourteen hours a day. That's a long time to work.

I quickly learned the bell system. Every time a bell rang, the children would have to take a specific action for the day to run smoothly. We were not allowed to be late, tardy, or give an excuse that we didn't hear the bell, even if we were doing chores in the barn. The farm manager always watched the time to get the chore boys up to the building for meals.

The first bell in the morning was at 6:00 a.m. We'd wake up, get dressed, make our beds, wash our faces, and brush our teeth. The next small bell rang lightly, not like the long, one-minute bell. It would alert us to rush to the chapel for announcements, prayers, and readings. Sometimes we had lectures on specific behaviors or topics.

After chapel, I rushed downstairs to the bottom floor to line up in the hallway that led to the dining room for breakfast. Food was always plentiful, and if you worked on your table mates, you could get extra food by trading out your afternoon snack. After breakfast, depending on how fast you ate your breakfast, you could spend more time playing in the playroom, which was located on the bottom floor down the hall from the dining room.

The next bell was the school bell, which meant we all had to report to our classrooms that were located on the second floor behind the main staircase. The first classroom was run by Mrs. Larson, which went from kindergarten to fifth grade, with only one teacher. Fifth through eighth grades were located in the second classroom. I had two teachers in the three years I spent in that classroom.

The last teacher I had was during seventh grade. She got married on Valentine's Day in the chapel upstairs, which was a special day for the whole school to attend a wedding with bridesmaids. Of course, some of the bridesmaids were also students.

When the lunch recess bell rang, which was one of the best bells of the day, we all rushed out of the classroom and ran down the outside steel staircase to the playground. We had free play until the lunch bell rang. The boys went to the boys' playground, and the girls went to the girls' playground. At lunch, we reported to the dining room hallway again. The big thing was that we had to wash our hands and go through a hand inspection given by one of the staff members at the dining room door. A lot of us boys had very chapped hands and wrists, because when we went to wash our hands, there were no towels to wipe our hands dry. After awhile, we learned to put our hands under our armpits to dry them off on our shirts. Of course, our wrists never got dry and they became severely chapped. Sometimes my wrists would break open and bleed because of the chapping. Sometimes a matron would put cream on our wrists and hands before bedtime.

We were allowed free play on the playground or down in the playroom at the end of the hall after lunch, until the school bell rang again for the afternoon sessions. The next bell was the most exciting bell of the day. It meant school's out. We could do or go anywhere we wanted to, until we heard the supper bell, which rang long and loud around 5:00 p.m. We'd drop everything we were doing and go to the downstairs hallway. We'd quickly wash our hands, go to the bathroom, and then get in line before the hand inspection at the dining room door. We would try to eat as fast as we could to get outside and continue to play.

The 7:00 p.m. bell was the East Room signal telling us to report upstairs and get ready for bed. The 8:00 p.m. bell alerted the West Room boys and girls to go upstairs and get ready for bed. The nine o'clock bell was for the Big West Room boys and girls, but they got a short bell for a warning. Then fifteen minutes later, they had a long bell to let them know that they were late getting to their dormitory. The older boys and girls had to be in by 11:00 p.m., unless they were attending an in-town high school function.

Yes, we heard a lot of bells ringing, but we got used to which bells were for us.

When everyone went to bed, prayers were said every night, and we were instructed if we didn't talk, the matron would read us a story. Half of us would fall asleep during the story.

Middle-of-the-night sounds would come from someone who was having nightmares. The boy would wake up crying for his mommy or he'd say things such as, "No, Daddy, no Daddy." Sometimes I would wake up hearing the sounds, and it made the nights seem scary when I was in the East Room. Some nights the matron would come in, sit on the boy's bed, and quiet him down until he could go back to sleep. There was a lot of silent crying and sniffles from someone wanting their mommy, but they didn't talk about it the next morning.

I learned to cry silently with tears running into my ears as I lay there staring at the ceiling. I didn't want the other boys to call me a sissy. There were many evenings when I fell asleep with tears in my ears. I also would learn to crawl into my friend's bed when I got scared in the middle of the night. Those nights during a thunderstorm with lightning and loud thunder claps were the scariest nights of all because there were no light-restricting curtains on the dormitory room windows. All we had were sheer, see-through curtains. We would get up and pull the shades down, but it still looked like the lightning bolt was going to come right into my bed. Following the lightning was always a great big boom or crack. I knew that it had hit the side of the building, because we were on the third floor and it was the highest building around for miles—that's what the big kids said; therefore, it must be true.

Keeping all those boys and girls in clean clothing was organized with a specific method. Every boy got two pairs of blue, button-up-the-front coveralls when we were small boys in the East Ward. The other boys got two pairs of jeans to wear, and we kept all our clothes in a tall, green locker, which was at the end of the bedroom. Separating the two rows of beds along each wall were three, long benches in the middle of the room. I would sit down, take my shoes and socks off, and put my dirty socks down in the bottom of my locker.

My locker had a number on it, which matched the number stenciled on the inside of my coveralls. My socks had my locker number stenciled on the bottom. I had a net canvas bag in my locker and I had to place all my dirty clothes in that bag on laundry day, which was Monday and Thursday.

Most of my daily shirts were cotton striped with long sleeves. When boys were in the East Room, (five to seven years old) every boy had white cotton T-shirts during the summer months, and we had two heavy wool plaid shirts for the winter. The West Room (eight-to twelve-year-olds) had only three cotton T-shirts for the summer and cotton long-sleeved plaid shirts for winter wear.

All the boys had a winter jacket issued to them, along with gloves, stocking caps, and black, seven-buckle rubber boots. Our winter clothes stayed downstairs in our lockers in the room across the hall from the playroom. The end of the hallway led to a staircase that went up and outside to the playground. The younger boys had to wear mittens. I found out awfully quick that I wanted gloves. I could make better snowballs with gloves than I could with mittens. Mittens got wet quicker than cotton gloves, and I would have to come in sooner because my hands kept getting numb and frostbitten.

I kept my Sunday going-to-church clothes on the other side of my locker in the bedroom. Each boy had one white cotton shirt with a collar, along with one pair of dark blue dress slacks and a pair of black shoes. I knew the black lace-up shoes had been somebody else's, and he had grown out of them. The toes were scuffed and re-polished downstairs on the shoe room's buffing machine.

The art of controlling all those kids was to put the fear of God to work. The orphanage was sponsored by the Trinity Evangelical Free Church of America, so religion was very strong in our daily lives. All of us were required to attend chapel every day after we had gotten dressed. The chapel was on the third floor, between the girls and boys dormitory at the top of the stairs. The chapel bell rang at seven o'clock every morning. Daily announcements were first on the agenda, followed by a prayer. There were two blackboards on either side of the stage, which had a quote from the Bible written on it. We were required to read this quote, and we had to remember something about the quote. The superintendent would give a little sermon connected to the quote. The head matron and the superintendent would sometimes ask us a question about the quote during the day.

"What did you learn from the quote this morning?"

We were expected to give some kind of statement in regards to the scripture. If we couldn't come up with a statement, we would get reprimanded with no mid-morning or mid-afternoon snack, regardless of the time it was that they asked the question.

Following the small sermon would be one or two more prayers, which were to help us get through the day. Sometimes, my prayers didn't last all day and I'd do something I was not supposed to be doing. One example was trying to kiss girls in the little park located behind the superintendent's house. At other times, I and a group of boys would throw clods at cars traveling on the main road as they passed the front driveway. One day, we put gasoline from the farm pump into the irrigation ditch that flowed through the alfalfa field into the cornfields. Why or how we obtained matches, I don't know, but it was fun to light that gasoline and see how far it would go down the irrigation ditch.

There were so many things to distract us from God. That is why we got a little sermon every morning from the superintendent or head matron, Minnie Johnson.

Minnie was the head matron, and she had been at the home for twenty years before I arrived. She was short, had wide shoulders, and a body like a wrestler. Her hair was braided and always wrapped around to the front of her forehead. It was held in place by a beaded clasp. She always wore dark, short-sleeved dresses that exposed her upper arms, which were as thick as a farm hand's arm. Besides that, she had a wrestler's grip on her right hand. She played favorites, and a number of the girls were her pets. However, she didn't like boys. Minnie knew boys were always after her girls, and she and her staff had to protect the girls.

Our Sunday mornings always consisted of church. The intention was to keep young children's minds from having bad thoughts and it helped us avoid temptations. Sunday morning was dress-up day, and we would have chapel before breakfast. Then, after breakfast, we were all loaded onto the yellow bus and driven into town to the church for Sunday school. After Sunday school, we attended the Sunday sermon.

We all sat in a group with guards at each corner of the pews. The rule was no talking or poking. If you did, you would get the evil eye of the matrons or the office personnel sitting in the corner of the pews. If you kept on poking or talking, that afternoon you would have to see Minnie Johnson in her room. Bulldog Minnie wasn't afraid to give anyone a couple of whacks on the butt with her big paddle that had holes as big as Chinese checker marbles.

According to the big boys, the paddle stung terribly when it made contact. She kept the paddle in her office on the wall next to her desk. She rarely used it, but we always knew it was there. She mainly gave me a lecture and twisted my ear as she talked. She wanted yes and no for answers. I found out quickly to speak loudly since shaking my head yes or no brought a whole lot of pain. One trick I had was to start showing big tears as I whimpered, which made the lecture shorter and less painful. Bawling loudly caused her to twist your ear harder. The secret about how to work bulldog Minnie was given to me by the bigger boys who had been summoned to her office over the years.

Most punishments by other staffers meant no lunch or dinner when we were caught doing something wrong during the day. Some staffers' punishments called for reporting to the matron upstairs in the dormitory. When that happened to me, I would have to go to bed without dinner. If I were treating another boy with destructive behavior, and the staff personnel caught me, they would have me report to the superintendent or maintenance man, who would then give me a paddling and send me to bed.

When you became eight years old at the orphanage, you were assigned a job or chores to carry out, before and/or after school.

Mondays and Thursdays were laundry days. On those days, I would take all my dirty socks, along with my coveralls and place them in the little bag. I would take the metal pin with my number on it and close the bag so it wouldn't open. After I dressed, brushed my teeth, and combed my hair, I returned to my room. I took the sheets off my bed, picked up my laundry bag, and carried them both to the hallway, where there were two huge gray canvas hampers. I tossed each article into the hampers designated for each article. The boys assigned to laundry duty for that week pushed the hampers to the laundry room, after they attended chapel and before breakfast.

The laundry room was located on the third floor, behind the chapel. The boys and girls who had laundry duty for the week worked in the laundry room after school. The washing machines could handle about one-hundred pounds of clothing per each washing cycle. After twenty to thirty minutes of washing, the huge machines would go into a spin cycle to pull a lot of water out of the clothing. The clean clothes from the washers were emptied into gray hampers, and then pulled to an upright top-loaded ringer. After the hundred pounds of clean clothing were loaded into the ringer, with the lid closed, the ringer would spin at a great rate of speed, drawing out the excess water.

The next procedure was to take the spun-dried clothes out of the ringer, and place them into another hamper; then it was rolled over to the tumble dryer. This machine was a huge commercial dryer that had gas burners at the bottom of the dryer. The load of sheets were placed into a hamper after coming out of the ringer and then rolled over to the corner of the laundry room. Once there, a large steam-powered sheet mangle would be employed. It took four girls to operate this part of the folded sheets. The front two girls pulled the sheets apart out of the hamper, spread the sheet by the corners, and placed the corners onto the front rollers of the mangle.

As the sheet wound its way through the many rollers of the mangle, it came out the back end, nice and pressed. The back two girls would take the sheets from the rollers, fold the sheets, and then stack them into a gray, wheeled hamper. The boys pushed the hampers full of sheets back through the chapel to the dormitories. At the bed bell, I went upstairs and before getting into bed, I pulled back the bedspread and made my bed before I got dressed and ready for bed.

On Tuesdays and Fridays, we had ironing duties. Minnie Johnson assigned specific girls to those tasks. The girls would work in a room on the second floor that had ten ironing boards. The girls would iron the girls' white blouses along with the boys' white Sunday school shirts. On one or two days throughout the month, tablecloths and other clothing articles were run through the mangle for pressing.

Wednesday was patch day, which was done in the same second-story room behind the classrooms. In this room, there were four sewing machines along with the ironing boards. Four staff members did the sewing. They would put patches on coveralls and jeans, and would mend knee and pocket tears.

Ripped front pockets on Sunday school shirts, and back pockets of jeans were always a problem until Levi started putting brass eyelets on the corners of the back pockets. There were special work situations at different times of the year where all the kids would have to help. In the fall, all the kids who could walk were loaded up on the three hay wagons that were pulled by tractors or a pickup. They took us to a huge forty-acre potato field to pick potatoes. The boys and girls would walk on either side or at the back of the wagons, picking up the freshly dug up potatoes from the ground. We would throw the potatoes into the back of the wagon. When the wagons were full of potatoes, they were driven to the root cellar located on the side of the boy's playground.

The wagons would go to the entrance of the root cellar. A conveyor belt ran down into the root cellar. Inside were four tiers of shelving made from wire mesh fencing. They were located across the middle of the shelf and nailed to the wooden frames, in four tiers, approximately 200 yards long. The older kids were instructed to spread the potatoes out on those shelves to keep the potatoes for the winter months. The potatoes were also stored with other vegetables, such as turnips, beets, and winter cabbage. Big blue fruit jars with canned vegetables and tomatoes were stored in the cellar for winter usage as well.

Another event occurred when the matrons would have all the children strip their beds of sheets and open all the windows on the south side of their bedrooms. Next, the older boys were asked to start pitching mattresses out the windows. They would let them fall two stories to the grass on the front yard. Other boys on the grass would place all the mattresses on the front yard to air out. After lunch or one o'clock in the bright sunshine, the boys would flip the mattresses over to get the sunshine to shine on the other side of the mattresses.

On one of the mornings when I was nine years old, I got a bright idea when I saw the boys throwing the mattresses out the window. I talked to some of the kids in the yard who were stacking the mattresses four or five high. As they got a tall stack of mattresses, I ran up the stairs and sat on the windowsill above the high-stacked mattresses. I hollered down for them to give me the count of mattresses. As they got to five high, I sat out on the window sill, and it looked scary.

I said, "Pile on two more mattresses."

When they got to seven, I stood up on the windowsill and jumped two stories. I landed on the mattresses flat on my back. I knew enough to lie flat out to land on my back. Once I did this, the other boys started following what I had just done.

We used the word "Jiggers" as the signal that the authority was right around the corner, as the matron Lori came into the room to check how the process was going. The boys in the room started pitching more mattresses out of the other windows in the room. She couldn't understand why so many boys were running up the stairs all morning. Finally, she went over to the window and saw the stack of mattresses. She then put a stop to all the fun we were having and stayed in the room to oversee the last mattress being tossed out the window.

Another fun sport during the spring and fall was when the big boys were to chop off chickens' heads. The other children were supposed to dunk the chickens in hot water and pull off the feathers. The next group of children were instructed to burn the pinfeathers off the chickens. The staff would then cut the chickens and prepare them for the freezer storage, which would feed the kids for the summer and winter months. There were 150 to 200 chickens processed on those special days.

The best part was to watch the boys who chopped off the chicken's head. They would sharpen their axes and look for old tree trunks that had been placed around the bus barn. They would grab the chickens by the feet, lay their heads across the tree trunk, and slam the ax down on the chicken's neck. As soon as that happened, the boys would throw the chickens out in the yard. Most of those chickens would start running through the yard with blood shooting out of their necks. Of course, blood was all over the other boys who were trying to run with those headless chickens. There was always loud laughter and shouts of, "I dare you."

Being a grade AAA dairy farm and having 280 acres of land, the orphanage needed the boys' help. Everyday chores were carried out by the boys who had to work in the milking barn. The working of the land and harvesting needed a lot of boy power. The farm manager,

Mr. Honeywell, was in charge of running the dairy barn and farming the land. He and his family of two girls—one girl was my age—lived in a little single-story house on the road to the dairy barn. The Honeywell's house was located approximately 300 yards south of the main house. We spent a lot of time at the Honeywell's on Wednesdays after school. She had Bible study on her front porch, and of course, she served homemade cookies.

Mr. Wessman, the superintendent, gave me my first and best job, when I was seven years old. He asked me to help his family with various chores on Wednesdays and Saturdays.

Mr. Wessman and his family consisted of two girls and his wife, Martha, who was very pretty. She was always interested in the things I did in school. I never had anybody interested in anything I did. So, she was special. My first job was to carry trash cans into the garage and empty them into a barrel. Then I had to roll the barrel down the driveway on Saturday mornings. The older boys with a pickup truck would come to take the barrel, and they would burn the contents in the incinerator that was located on the boys' playground.

After I brought the trashcans back into the house, Mrs. Wessman would give me other minor chores. Sometimes she would have me move things, sweep the front steps, or do any other little chores she needed completed. After two weeks of performing my job, she asked me to come over on Saturday morning after I had my breakfast. After about a month of this, her two daughters were speaking to me and they wanted me to come over on Saturdays to help the cleaning girl, Dixie, who came to clean their house.

I helped with the vacuuming and moved lamps and small tables that were too heavy for the girls to move. I did dusting and other chores, and most tasks were completed by noon. This was when Mrs. Wessman would ask if Dixie and I wanted to stay and have lunch with the two girls. Of course, I knew not to decline food that would almost certainly be better than what we would get at the dining hall.

Dixie and I would stay all afternoon. We played with the two sisters and listened to the radio. We had no TV in the early 40s. My favorite radio shows were the *Adventures of Straight Arrow, Sky King,* and the *Adventures of Roy Rogers*. I got to be a fixture in the Wessman's house for the girls begged Martha, their mother, to have me come over for breakfast on my chore days. Those breakfasts were the greatest breakfasts I had ever eaten. They rated second only to my mama's homemade cinnamon toast.

Mrs. Wessman made toast in the broiler oven and then cut a round hole in the center of that toast with a round cookie cutter. She then would put a poached egg in the center and poured hot maple syrup over the whole thing. What a treat that was for me! I didn't know what a poached egg was. I had never seen one.

Eating eggs in the orphanage dining room area for breakfast was a different thing. Most of the time, I got scrambled eggs. When I did get fried eggs, the yellow yolk was always hard and bright yellow. The platter had eggs piled ten to twelve high, usually amounting to thirty to forty eggs. Therefore, I could take two or three at a time. I would take my three and then eat Stanley Steamer's two eggs, because he hated fried eggs.

My next job at eight years old was to go to the barn in the morning and help with feeding the hogs and caring for the sows. In the springtime, the sows were giving birth to baby piglets. We had big heat lamps hanging from the rafters over the sow as she gave birth to keep the piglets from freezing from the night air. The pig crew consisted of four to five boys. They had to watch the sows and piglets day and night. The piglets were separated from the mama sow right after being born. Some sows would try to eat their litter or try to find the runt of her litter. She would get rid of the small piglet by eating it. We had to watch the mama sow as she went to lie down in the pen. She would sometimes lie on the piglets.

We had to put a 2 x 4 gate across the pen to keep the piglets on one side of the fence and the sow, lying down on the other side. The piglets could get to the sows for feeding. We would not let the sow get to the piglets. We also had to watch out for the runt of the litter and make sure we could get him to the nipple so he could eat. The other piglets would not let the little runt have access to the nipple. They kept pushing him away. He didn't grow to his full size because he couldn't eat properly. Our job was to take the runt and put him to a nipple, while keeping all the other little pigs away from him while he ate as much as he could. Some of the boys would take turns throughout the night to watch the birthing of the piglets. We tended the heat lamps hanging over the pens in the pig barn so the piglets would not get cold and die.

Every two to three weeks we had to clean out the twenty-five pigpens on a Saturday morning. We had to pitch out the old straw that had a lot of pig manure and other nasty things in it. It was very heavy on the end of the pitchfork. The pig crew and I had to pick up this nasty stuff and we would gag when we first started. We would pick up the stinking straw and pitch it into an old manure spreader. That machine would spread the old manure over the hay fields as a tractor pulled it through the fields.

There was a wooden seat at the front of the manure spreader where the driver would sit when the machine was pulled by horses. However, now we were pulling it with a tractor. Roger Dodger found out that the faster the tractor went while out in the hay field, the higher in the air the maneuver would fly. In fact, if they went too fast on the tractor, it would make the manure fly up to the front of the spreader, hitting the people on the wooden seat.

One Saturday, we got Stanley Steamer and Mustard to sit on the seat. We gave them the job of pulling the lever that was on the left side of the green wagon. Pulling the lever backwards engaged the double teeth in the back of the wagon to start rotating and it would throw the manure out onto the field as the wagon moved. I was riding the fender on the tractor because I was supposed to be the signal man.

My job was usually to pull back the lever, and then get back on the tractor fender. I would watch the spreading of the manure, and if something got caught in the rotating teeth of the spreader, I was supposed to alert the driver to stop the tractor. We stopped at the alfalfa field, and I hollered to Stanley Steamer and Mustard to pull the lever backwards. I then told them to hold on, and we started moving across the alfalfa field. I told the driver to make the tractor go faster. The maneuver and wet straw started flying high in the air.

Steamer and Mustard were sitting on the seat, holding onto the sides of the seat as the wagon bounced across the field. They were watching me as I told them to watch my arms for the signal to push the lever forward, which would disengage the manure spreader. I turned to Roger Dodger and I told him to go faster. At that moment, the manure started hitting Steamer and Mustard on the back of the head and plastered the backs of their jackets. They started cussing and waving their hands as we got to the end of the field. We had to slow down and turn to go back towards the barn. Steamer and Mustard jumped from the seat and started after us. However, by that time, we had turned around and started towards the barn. They had to walk back to the barn with straw and manure falling off their jackets. Things like this happened all the time.

My next job at age nine was to go to the barn in the mornings with the big boys, before breakfast. The boys took care of the milking, and Sterling and I were to take care of the weaned calves. The calves were approximately eight weeks old. There were three or four buckets that hung on the top board of the fence that surrounded the calves located in the milking barn. Those buckets had rubber nipples on one side of the bucket. We had to pour warm milk into the bucket, and then we had to get the little calves to start sucking the rubber nipple to get the milk into their mouths.

We first had to get the calves to suck with their tongues. We had to take our forefingers, stick our fingers in the calf's mouth, and get them to suck our fingers. The first time I had to put my fingers in a calf's mouth, I thought the calf would bite me, or butt me with his head because he was as tall as I was. I jammed my fingers in his mouth, moved my fingers in and out of his mouth, and the calf automatically started sucking my fingers. Once the calf started to suck my fingers, I could lead him around in the pen to the buckets with the rubber nipples. I got to the bucket with the calf following me. I brought my hand and the calf's mouth to switch to the long rubber nipples. This is how we got the calves to suck on the rubber nipple of the bucket to get their milk.

Since the dairy barn was an AAA-grade milking barn, we had to keep the barn as clean as possible to pass state inspections. After each milking, we had to scoop out the cow manure, which had fallen in two concrete troughs that ran the length of the barn on each side of the walkway. The stalls were on both sides of the barn, so there were two troughs to clean. With a wide-scoop shovel, the boys pushed the manure out into the barnyard. They would have to hose down the barn after each milking with water hoses.

Once the white lime was on the barn floors, we would bring alfalfa hay down from the top floor of the barn called the hayloft. They would drop the alfalfa down through chutes, which were located at the sides of the hayloft. The boys would pitch the hay with a pitchfork into the head rack, which was at the head of the stall. This is how they kept milk cows calm, while the boys milked. Some cows had to have little metal kick guards chained around their back legs to keep them from kicking the stainless steel bucket.

On Saturdays, we had to wash down the entire barn, and then we would put lime on the floors. This was to kill all the bacteria and germs from getting into the milk. We had periodical inspectors from the state visits us. They did their testing to find out how clean our barn, equipment, and milk rooms were. Everything had to meet state standards to be AAA milk. Sometimes after an inspection, we had to wash and white lime the barn down every night until we passed inspection.

The milking crew had to milk the cows morning and evenings. They had the most modern vacuum air-milking canisters throughout the whole barn. This allowed the crew to hook up the milker's suction tubes to the cow's tits, which automatically sucked on the cow's tits. The milk went into a stainless steel enclosed bucket, which was hooked to a belt and was placed around the cow's stomach.

After milking each cow, the crew member carried the stainless steel container to the front of the barn and put it into the milk room. We had to pour the fresh raw milk from the milking canister into a large square stainless steel tank, called the holding tank. The next step was to process the milk through a machine called a separator, which spun out three kinds of milk, such as, skim milk, whole milk, and cream. A third of the milk that was produced daily went to the house to be given to the children. The excess milk went into five-gallon milk cans. It was picked up via the dairy truck that came to the barn every other day. That skim milk was used to slop the hogs every morning.

We had jobs to do as we grew up in the orphanage. However, we learned responsibility, and we learned how to work with each other, which was a good thing.

Having lived in a Christian children's home has taught me that I had a guardian angel to help me through life when things were not going in the right direction. As a child, I knew there was somebody looking over me. Praying to God got me through a lot of rough times as well as good times.

As an orphan boy, you learn to always have two things—hope that each day will be filled with something nice, even though sometimes you have to look for it, and peace with everyone you meet until they show their true colors. Words are easy to come by, but actions speak louder than words.

Chapter 8

Learning to Have Fun as An Orphan Boy

Learning to live happily without Mama and my grandpa in my life every day was certainly an adjustment I had to make. For a long time I silently kept hoping Mama or Papa would show up and take me home. As the years went by, and Papa only came for visits or to take me home with him for a few weeks, I learned this was my new way of life. I could either spend it feeling sad and crying, or I could realize there was nothing I could do to change my circumstances.

As I spent more time in prayer and at the chapel everyday with the other boys, I decided I needed to learn how to have fun as an orphan boy.

Our entertainment had a lot to do with the seasons of the year. In the winter months, we spent a lot of time playing basketball in the playroom, which had a nine-foot ceiling. Instead of a basket ball hoop that guys could hang on, we had a painted square on the wall.

The younger boys would wait until the older boys were finished with their basketball games. Then we'd take shots at playing PIG, but none of us could hit the square on the wall because it was too high up. But we had fun developing our ball-bouncing skills.

Sometimes we would do things that got us in trouble. One time I put broken crayons into metal lids that came off cocoa tins or tea containers. We had found the tea containers on the boy's playground in the fire pit where the garbage was burned every day. Then I'd place the lid on the steam radiators located on the window side of the playroom. I would wait about twenty minutes until the crayons melted. The trick was to pick up the hot tin lid, carry it out in the hall, up the stairs, and out onto a snowbank where the hot tin could cool down. That was how I found out that I could use my brown mittens to pick up the hot tin off the radiator. Spilling the melted crayons all over the black tiled floor was another lesson to learn. I had to scrape the hardened crayons off the floor, and I had to use a borrowed pocketknife or a skate key to save the hardened wax.

After placing the tin in a snowbank, I would run back to the playroom, since I was freezing from going outside without a coat or boots. As soon as I got back, I would start on a second tin. I would finish setting up the second tin on the radiator, and then I'd run outside to find my cooled tin. I turned the tin upside down and slammed it on the concrete. Instantly, the hard crayon disk would fall out of the tin. I'd then go inside and compare my creation with the other boys' designs. We'd then decide who had the best-looking design.

Another challenge in the playroom during the winter was high jumping. Someone would get a rope from his locker that he had found at the barn or the bus barn. He would bring it back as one of his prized possessions and store it in his locker. The boy became a hero because of that fact. I always had a rope in my locker, because I was Lash LaRue, the cowboy who had a bullwhip around his shoulder. I would take the bad guys down by snapping the guns out of their hands or wrapping the bad guys around their legs. But, I wouldn't let the boys use my rope for high jumping. I was afraid I'd never see it again.

The older boys tied the rope to the hot water pipe that came down from the ceiling to the steam radiators, which sat on the floor, side by side, along the outside wall. To start the contest, all the boys would line up in a single file, and then they'd run to jump the rope, as it was only knee-high. As everybody made the first jump, the rope went up higher, and it kept getting higher. To be eliminated, all you had to do was miss one time. The first one eliminated would hold the other end of the rope.

As the rope got higher, the older boys would have us little guys go get our winter coats from across the hall. We'd pile the coats on the floor on one side of the rope. When the boys started to fall hard on the floor as the rope went higher, the coats provided something soft to land on to break their fall. Soon, the big boys were getting to the far end of the room, running as fast as they could to the rope. They would scissor-kick or barrel-roll over the rope.

Another game we played was Peg Ball. Somebody always had a small rubber ball that they had gotten for Christmas and had stashed in their locker. The object of the game was for everybody in the room to keep away from having the ball hit them. If you got hit by the ball, then you'd have to run after the ball, pick it up, and throw it at another boy. You would try to hit him before you had to leave the room. Most times, I lasted only through half of the game before I got hit.

One of the things that we looked forward to on Saturday mornings was our morning snack. During the winter, we would get apples, sometimes oranges, or maybe a square of coffeecake. If it was freezing outside and there was snow on the ground, I would make an orange crush. I would throw the oranges up against the playroom walls, and catch them before they hit the ground. I threw them just hard enough to soften the orange on the inside. Some boys would throw it too hard and it cracked the orange's skin. Then they would have to eat it right away. I would work the oranges with my hands to release the juices inside without breaking the skin of the orange.

Next, I would get my winter coat and boots on to go outside in the snowstorm or cold winds. I took my orange along with other friends' oranges. I would trudge through the deep snow and blowing winds to get behind the bus barn, sometimes walking backwards to keep my face out of the wind. I could always find snow drifts, which were deep around the south side of the barn. Finding a snowbank without letting anyone see where I placed the oranges was another reason for walking backwards. Before snack time the next day, I would retrieve the frozen oranges. I then carried all the oranges into the playroom. I would take my orange and throw it hard against the wall of the playroom. It would crack and splinter into many pieces. I hurried and grabbed the pieces of frozen orange and sucked on them to drink the cold juice. What a great dessert for all the hard labor.

When the snow melted several days later, I could go out early in the morning and find ten or twenty oranges and apples lying on the ground. Many of the kids forgot where they had stashed their apples or oranges during the storm.

Another thing we'd do in the winter was go out to the swings on the playgrounds right after a severe snowstorm. The wind during a snowstorm would blow between the car barn, where the staff parked their cars, and the bus barn, to the point that the snow blew into a huge snow drift in front of the swings. The ground underneath the swings had very little snow coverage. The top of the swings was at least twelve feet high. When you started pumping in a swing to the top peak, you were probably ten feet off the ground. The snowbanks in front of the swings could reach five to eight feet high, depending on the severity of the storm.

Later on in the day, we would make a slide on the other side of the snow drift, facing away from the swings. The slide was made by riding a scoop shovel down the slope of the snowbank many times during the day. In the late afternoon, we would find a bucket of water and pour cold water on the slide's indentation. The next day it would be a fast ride down the snowbank when I jumped off the swing. This is why it is great to have older brothers to show you the tricks of being a boy.

Another great thrill was when the farm manager, Mr. Honeywell, would get the little gray Ford tractor and chain a huge sheet, at least fifteen feet long of corrugated roofing material behind the tractor. He would pull this corrugated material out onto the alfalfa field and put twenty to thirty boys and girls on the metal sheet. All the boys and girls would sit behind each other and wrap their arms around the person in front of them, trying to hang onto each other. Mr. Honeywell would start pulling the sheet across the snow. When he got to the middle of the alfalfa field covered with fresh soft snow, he would make a sharp turn, which caused the sheet metal to go faster as it slid around the outside of the turn. Most of the boys and girls would roll off the metal sheet into the deep snowbanks at the end of the alfalfa field. He would stop the tractor, let everybody climb aboard, and then he would pick up the speed before he would turn. After about five or six rollovers, he would go faster and turn in the opposite direction. Expecting to roll off in a specific direction, he would trick us. We rolled in the opposite direction and tumbled over each other into the snow. I was having a lot of fun

Spring brought new life to the trees as well as green fields. The smell of turning over dark, rich soil behind the plows was in the air as the tractor kept going back and forth through the fields. We'd retrieve our bats and baseballs from the boys lockers, and we would drag the baseball diamond with a homemade leveler. The leveler was square and made out of two-by-fours with heavy metal fence nailed to the bottom. Two or three small kids would get on the square and the bigger boys would pull them around the baseline. This removed all the rocks and smoothed out the dirt, for better baseball. We made bases out of gunnysacks filled with the pea gravel shoveled off the boys' play area.

After school, there was not enough time to choose teams to play a regular nine-inning baseball game, because the sun would go down before the supper bell. We played a game called the "Workup," which allowed all of us to play, no matter what our age or playing skills were.

One time while I was in left field, the batter hit a ball to me. I got my brown gloves up in front of my face. I followed the ball into my hands. The ball hit my gloved hands, slipped through, and hit me in the forehead. I fell to the ground unconscious. All the players ran over to me and gathered around. Someone ran to get a wet rag and placed it on my forehead. When I woke up a couple minutes later, I had a wet cloth on my forehead and one on the back of my neck. I got to my feet, but the big boys wouldn't let me play anymore that day. That incident ended my baseball career.

In the springtime, out on the plains, the wind blew strong day and night. We could depend upon it being windy every day in Nebraska. The older boys showed us how to build a kite out of the wooden crates that apples and oranges came in during the winter. We would split the wood and make crosses out of the slivers of wood.

Some boys would pool their money to buy a big roll of string with their allowance for kite-flying purposes. To make a kite, we'd take the string and wrap it around the center of the kite, fastening the two sticks together into a cross. Holding the string, after you have a notch at the tip of each stick, you would pull the string from notch to notch, getting it as tight as you could. This made a triangle-shaped outline.

Then, we would find old newspapers and paste them around the strings after we cut the newspaper an inch bigger than the triangle. We would paste the paper, then turn the paper over the string as tight as we could get it. The schoolteachers or office staff would usually give us the white paste.

The most important part of building a kite depended upon the next step. You had to take a string and tie it to the short stick of the triangle. Then you had to pull the opposite side of that stick up to a point so it acted as a bow. We'd wrap the other end of the string around that end to keep the bow taunt. Next, you would turn the kite over so the paper was on the top, and then you'd need to punch a hole in the paper at the crossbars. Finally, you would place your kite string through that hole and tie it to the crossbar.

To make a kite tail, we would go upstairs in the laundry room and find an old sheet to rip into long strips. Next, we would tie the strips to each other, and then attach them to the bottom part of the kite, which made the tail of the kite. The kite would fly straight up as it caught the wind. You had to gauge the links of your tail to the strength of the wind blowing.

I had two friends—Freddie, who we called the "Digger," and Stanley, who we called "Steamer." We wanted to build a huge kite, and Steamer found a straight stick four feet long and a cross stick that was three feet long.. That Saturday, we walked to town and bought six rolls of string. Saturday afternoon, we put the kite up in the air and had to keep adding a tail to it so that it would balance against the strong winds. The tail must have been fifteen feet long, but it kept the kite from wagging side to side.

Next, we started flying the kite, and we let the string out with a short broomstick through the cardboard's spool of string. When we got to the end of the first roll of string, we tied the second spool to the first one. The kite was already 1,000 feet out, and it looked very small. If we let the string out too fast through our hands, the weight of the string and the pull of the wind gave us string burns. We had to keep both hands tight on the string as we let the string out. Stanley Steamer ran to the downstairs locker room and got his cotton gloves at my request. He held the string while it was wrapped around his gloved hand, while I tied the next row of string to the previous string. We continued doing this until the kite was out of sight. We didn't have to run or walk forward to make the kite go up or down, because the wind was so strong. The kite flew all day Saturday. We took turns holding the kite string. On Saturday night, we tied the string to a fence post and when the bed bell rang, we all went upstairs to bed.

Every few hours, one of us would get up, sneak downstairs, and go out to the fence post. We would place our hands on the string to make sure the kite was still up. The kite stayed up for three days and three nights. In our minds, we had bragging rights for being the best kite flyers in the state of Nebraska.

The spring season brought out the engineering minds of the bigger boys who were going to build four-wheeled soapbox cars. Wheels came off some old red wagon, along with the axles to make soapbox cars. Finding a 2 x 4 long enough for the front wheels was easy when we looked through the old barn that had blown down a couple of years ago. The length was important to turn the front wheels without the wheels hitting the body of the soapbox car. We took the red wagons and axles, and nailed them to the 2 x 4. We bent the nails over the axles and pounded the nail heads into the 2 x 4 to keep the axle secured. We used a shorter 2 x 4 for the back wheels. Then, we attached the little red wagon wheels on the axles by putting a nail through the hole at the tip of the axle. Again, using the old orange crates sawed in half, we nailed it to the 2 x 4 over the back wheels. This served as the seat. Using a regular orange crate, we nailed it to the front of the cart along with two tin cans for headlights, which made it look like a real racer. We made approximately three to four carts every spring. The concrete driveway on the west side of the home was the Annapolis speedway.

The chore boys nailed a long rope to the front of the soapbox cart. Then, a couple of the boys sat in the back of the pickup, holding onto the rope. They pulled the cart from the home to the barn. It was approximately a quarter of a mile of dirt roads with a lot of potholes. This happened during the afternoon milking time.

I was nine years old when the chore boys tried to pull carts down the road that led to the barn. Most of the carts lost their wheels, and axles came off because of the bumpy dirt road. Sometimes a boy driving the cart was too heavy. When the racer would hit a pothole in the road, nails and axles would start falling off the 2 x 4's.

Bud Exstrom approached me and asked me to ride, because I was a small guy and a daredevil. Bud had me put on a stocking cap, cotton gloves, and kneepads that he had in his locker.

Milking time was around four o'clock in the afternoon. Bud had the soapbox tied behind the pickup with all the chore boys and we rode in the back of the truck and monitored the procedures. Blackie, the driver, after seeing that I was in the racer, got out of the driver's seat and started checking the steering with me. He had me pull the two ropes nailed to the long 2 x 4. I learned how to work the brakes on the soapbox racer. The brakes consisted of a broomstick nailed to the side of the 2 x 4 that was placed behind him and was pulled by the pickup truck. The broomstick was between my two skinny legs. If I wanted to stop, I had to pull the broomstick back, which dug into the ground underneath the soapbox. A second set of brakes was installed so I could dig my heels in the ground to stop.

Blackie started out slow and I was behind him in the pickup truck. Hitting the first pothole, nothing broke or fell off my racer. I guided the racer with the ropes tied to the front 2 x 4's. Blackie told me that when I would raise my hand higher than my head, the boys in the back of the pickup were to shout to Blackie, the driver, to go at a faster speed. Again, nothing fell off and I steered with the ropes, even though my face was thick with bellowing dust, as I picked up speed. I should have worn goggles but I didn't have any. I raised my hand again. Now I couldn't see the boys sitting on the tailgate of the pickup. There were a lot of wobbly vibrations and dipping into potholes, so I raised my hand again.

The boys began shouting out the speed as we traveled down the road—fifteen, now eighteen, twenty, and then twenty-two. When they got to twenty-five, we were in front of the barn running out of road. Then I realized the broomstick was not much help to stop the racer. The only way for me to stop was to drag my feet on the ground. There was no way that I was going to drag my feet going that fast.

The truck stopped, and I kept on going. The boys on the tailgate lifted their legs as the racer went under the tailgate. The soapbox hit the back bumper of the pickup truck. The orange crate smashed into a million pieces. The frame of the cart hit the axle of the truck with a sudden stop. I slid forward on the frame, which sent me traversing under the truck with the thick dust. It was impossible for me to see anyone, or for anyone to see me.

All the boys jumped off the bed of the truck and they thought I was dead. The dust cleared, and they looked under the pickup where I was lying on my back with dirt covering my entire body. I didn't move. Bud and Blackie jumped out of the front of the truck and climbed under the pickup truck.

They shouted, "Jimmy! Jimmy!"

I began moving, knocking off the splintered wood, and crawled out from under the truck.

Blackie hollered, "He's all right. He's all right."

The chore boys started to cheer and shouted, "Twenty-five miles an hour; twenty-five miles an hour."

They were all dusting me off as I stood up. I had scratches on both arms, and one of my pant's legs had ripped up the whole leg. That night, I found many splinters in my butt. I was a hero that day, but the adventure prompted me to think long and hard about ever riding a handmade cart again. Of course, we couldn't tell the farm manager, Mr. Honeywell, because we knew we would get in trouble. That night, I told the matron, Laura, that I had fallen off the big merry-go-round called "The Wave" that was located on the boys' playground. The Mercurochrome stung that night.

Another event for all the boys was getting haircuts. They would load us up on the yellow bus with all the boys to go into town on the last Wednesday of the month. All the barber shops would stay open, and the bus would go around town and drop eight or ten boys off at each of the three barbershops. Then, the bus would go back to the home and pick up another load of boys to exchange places with the boys coming from the barber shops. The younger boys would go first, since they had to be back before the early bed bell. All the barber chairs were full until all heads of hair were cut, which took about three hours.

I learned from the barber when I first got my haircut, at age five, to keep my head perfectly still. I would only move my head when the barber moved it. Most boys wiggled and turned in the chair because the hair tickled, or they were scared of the clippers. Some boys just didn't listen. When the barber bent my head right or left, I held that position until he told me to do something different. I tried to get the same barber every month. Since I sat so still, he would give me a nickel, and said that I was the best boy out of the bunch.

When fall arrived, the weather turned cold during the evenings. Those were great days to play football. Teams for tag football were chosen from the lineup, using the one, two, and three method. The number ones and the number twos were lined up as the two main teams. Captains of the number one and number two teams chose players for their teams from the number three boys.

In those tag football games, there was a lot of blocking and passing of the football. The quarterback could run with the ball only if the quarterback couldn't find anyone open for a pass. The quarterback would then run and try to get a first down. We had goal posts at either end of the field, which consisted of two, fifty-gallon empty barrels.

One day, I was chasing the runner and was going to tackle him. I guess I was yelling, for I had my tongue out. As I dove for him, the heel of his shoe caught my chin. I bit into my tongue, as we both fell to the ground. I came up yelling, but I couldn't speak since my tongue was hanging out of my mouth by a thread, and blood was all over my chin.

I ran to the farm manager's farmhouse, which was only twenty feet away. Banging and screaming at the front door brought Mrs. Honeywell outside to find out what was going on. She quickly rushed me into the kitchen and found a wet washcloth. She wrapped my tongue with the washcloth, and tucked the whole thing inside my mouth. I stopped crying, because I couldn't make any noise. Tears just flowed down my cheeks. Of course, the whole tribe of boys had followed me. Luckily, Mr. Honeywell was in the back of the house, and he called the superintendent, Mr. Larson, at the big house. He got into his car, drove to the farmhouse, and then he took me to the doctor.

The doctor said, "I can't stitch your tongue. The only thing I can do is tell you to keep your mouth shut and gargle with hydrogen peroxide."

I stayed in bed for three days and consumed liquids through a straw. I could only have milkshakes and warm soup. Sure enough, my tongue healed and I was soon back playing football again. I made sure my tongue was in my mouth and I didn't do any yelling when I played tag football for the remainder of the fall season.

Christmas is the highlight of the year in an orphanage. Three weeks before Christmas, the bus was loaded up with the children who were going to be in the Christmas pageant for the church. Some of us had parts in the Christmas play, while others had to sing in the choir, and both events depended upon our age group.

When I was three years old, I had to be the baby Jesus for the Christmas play. I didn't have to go to rehearsal until three days before the pageant. On the first afternoon of rehearsal, the director placed me into the crib on the stage. There were many strange four-legged creatures around the crib. I was supposed to lie very still in that wooden box on the floor.

The first day I screamed when they put me in that box called a crib. One of the home girls stood over the crib and talked to me. The second day I didn't cry, because the girl was with me. She was dressed with a sheet over her head and a staff in her hand. I kept popping my head up wanting to see what all the people were doing around me, but I was supposed to lie very still. The girl had to stand over me to keep me still. During the last rehearsal, the director gave me a lollipop, which I could suck on while lying very still in the box that whole afternoon.

When it came time for the real performance, the director placed a new shepherd, a home girl dressed as a shepherd, close to the crib to keep me in the manger with my lollipop that had a very short stick. This was the brightest star I had ever been.

At the beginning of November, packages began arriving at the orphanage via the mail delivery truck. Packages also started to pile up on the stage in the chapel, which we watched very closely during every morning sermon. When the stage started piling up in the back from one side to the other, anticipation began to mount among us kids.

All the children in the orphanage got to have three wishes, and they were published in the local Holdrege paper. Our wishes consisted of things like flashlights, ballpoint pens, basketballs, pocketknives, and other small things that meant a lot to a kid who had nothing. Combination locks became popular when I was nine years old. The reason for their popularity was that regular locks had keys that kept disappearing, and boys couldn't gain access to their private lockers in the playroom.

On December 1, a mail truck pulled up to the front steps of the orphanage. A delivery man would start unpacking the brown, paper-wrapped gifts, and sometimes gifts were wrapped in Christmas paper. We kids would watch him unload his truck from the third floor front windows. He would get help from staff members to unload the packages and bring them up the stairs. They would then place the packages on the stage in the chapel.

What was in that big, square box? What was in that flat, long box? Whose name was on the nametag for that gift? We were always trying to find names on packages as we stood at the top of the stairs watching the packages passing by on their way to the chapel. The anticipation of Christmas continued to build until the day of the church pageant.

The ride back to the home that evening was the night before Christmas, December 24. Anticipation and excitement filled our thoughts, since we would get to open the gifts that were on that stage. The packages were stacked to the ceiling, WOW! Hardly anyone slept that night. We were all too busy talking, wishing, and hoping for the next day to come quicker. Usually two to three trucks per day that were full of gifts arrived at the front steps two weeks before Christmas. What excitement, anticipation, and thankfulness we had for all the people who had read the local *Holdrege Herald*. We were also grateful for the contributions from the surrounding churches and gift-giving people of the world. Every child in the orphanage had such a wonderful Christmas. Most people cannot conceive how our hearts were filled with joy and love for each other as well as the world. Living in an orphanage was not a bad thing. It was a good thing. We just had to learn to accept our life and enjoy the happiness only we could create.

Looking back, when I reached the age of six, as an orphan, I strongly believed in Santa Claus. There were no mothers or fathers in many of our lives. We believed there was a real Santa Claus. If we needed proof, all we had to do was look at our chapel stage that was stacked high with Christmas gifts.

One afternoon, I was called to the superintendent's office. When I entered, I saw him and a lady I didn't know.

He said, "Jimmy, this lady lives in town and she wants to take you to town to buy you the chaps you wanted for Christmas. She got your name through the local newspaper."

Whoa! What a deal! I thought. "Yes, I will go with you," I told her.

I followed her to her car, and she opened the door for me. I climbed in the front seat next to her. I had not been in a car since riding in Papa's car two years ago. As we rode along, she started asking me questions. She tried to get me to interact with her in a conversation, but at the age of six, I didn't say much. I didn't know who she really was. She had so many questions for me as we drove up the long driveway to the main road. I started answering every question as quickly as I could, after looking at her. I could see that she was a very nice person. I even volunteered a question.

"What kind of work do you do?"

I got an answer, and then I went on to the next question.

"Do you have any boys?"

She started to answer, but by then, we had parked in front of the store. She turned off the motor, removed the key, and opened her door. I could smell her nice perfume. It reminded me of the same smell when my mother took me to the store. She came around to open my door. Her gaze was on me all the while and I got out to follow her. She took me by my arm and offered me her open hand. She had taken the glove off of her right hand. I placed my little hand inside her warm hand, and then she wrapped her fingers around my hand. She wanted to answer my last question, as we walked into the store.

She said to me, "I had a boy your same age, but last year he got sick and didn't get well."

I stopped and turned to her, and looked up into her face.

I said, "What was his name?"

She looked down at me with sadness in her eyes and said, "Jimmy."

We then continued walking into the toy department. We approached a lady behind the counter.

The woman who brought me to the store, said, "We want to look at chaps for cowboys."

I tried on two or three pairs of different colors and sizes.

The lady asked me, "Which chaps would you like to take home with you?"

I pointed to the dark brown rawhide chaps. She told the lady to put the brown chaps in a box. She then had the clerk show us to the boot department. The clerk put my foot in a big metal shoe with lines across it. Then she pushed a metal bar up to my big toe and said I needed size nine shoes. We looked at three to four pairs of cowboy boots.

The lady with me pointed to the black shiny boots and said, "We want to get those because they look so nice with brown chaps."

I said, "Wow! These are my first pair ever."

I had never been as close to heaven as I was that day. I was so thrilled that I thought I would pee in my pants. I couldn't imagine riding the range with Roy Rogers (Bobby Broberg, my best friend, was Roy) and taking down all the bad guys.

The lady took me next door for a chocolate sundae, while the store clerk wrapped my gifts. Then the lady took my hand and we walked back to the store to get the packages. The two gifts looked huge to me. The paper was very shiny, and there were big bows on top of each gift. The lady let me carry one of the gifts. As she lowered it into my hands, I had to put out both my arms to carry it to the car. I was so thrilled and felt laughter in my heart. The lady had a smile from ear to ear, and I was so talkative all the way back to the home.

The lady gave the gifts to Mr. Larson's front office secretary. As we stood on the main floor, she bent down to get on an eye level with me to say goodbye. I wanted to hug the lady, I was so happy.

Instead, I looked her right in the eyes, and I said, "Thank you very much for my chaps and boots."

I don't know what made me say those words. There was no one in the orphanage or at Papa's who would have told me to say such words. The bell rang for dinner at that moment, so I turned, ran, and skipped down the hallway.

Opening gifts on Christmas Eve was the highlight of my year. First, we had to put on our best Sunday clothing and file down to the dining room, with no hand inspections at the door. We enjoyed a great dinner with mashed potatoes and brown gravy, which was hard to come by at our dinner table throughout the year. We only had mashed potatoes and gravy three or four times during the year.

After dinner, we would walk upstairs to the chapel. The stage that had been previously packed with gifts to the ceiling, and even out into the aisles before we had gone to dinner, was now empty. Again, we saw the picture of Jesus leaving the children in the picture, which was behind the pulpit.

We were filled with excitement and anticipation as we sat in the chapel that evening. We could barely sit still. We had our opening prayer and we listened to the Christmas sermon. Mr. Larson, the superintendent, then stood up.

He announced to everyone, "All the East Room boys and girls rise and go to your room."

The next group, who were from the West Room, were directed to go to their rooms. While we were at dinner, the matrons, along with other staff members, were upstairs in the chapel. After taking presents from the stage, the presents were delivered to the designated person's bed. Minnie Johnson had written names on the bottom of each present.

We walked into our room and on every bed—you couldn't see the beds because the gifts were piled high on each one. Each of the presents was gift-wrapped. There were no brown paper gifts, not like when they came in through the mail. For me, the gift pile was taller than I was.

That's when the screams and shouting started. All we could hear was the sound of wrapping paper being ripped off the gifts. After a few minutes, kids began shouting and asking for scissors or knives to cut strings or twine that had been wrapped around some of their gifts. I knew enough that the gifts with string or twine would be hard gifts to get into without a knife.

As the opened gifts became known, there would be shouts of "Wow" and "Yippee" in the air. The, "Hey, look what I got!" was screamed more than once. We would shout across our beds to the bedmate next to us. We couldn't see him because of the piled-high gifts and paper that filled the room. The gifts of wagons and bikes found a place at the foot of the kids' beds once the gifts were distributed. The activity of opening gifts went on for two hours.

After the boys showed their roommates and friends what they had received as gifts, the boys and girls started running across the hall to see what everybody else had received. The paper was flying through the rooms as the kids ran back and forth.

There was no bed bell that night for everybody. We could stay up late that night. Kids sat on their beds playing with the games, putting gifts together, or playing with flashlights that they had unwrapped. Finally, at midnight, the matron flicked the lights off and on, which meant that we had to get in our pajamas and get in bed.

She said, "Lights out in fifteen minutes."

Of course, the little guys in the East ward fell asleep before the lights were out. During the rest of the night with the lights out, the kids with flashlights were still going from room to room to see the presents that were the greatest.

This feeling of warmth and happiness was the greatest that could be experienced for boys and girls who never had the love of a mother or father at Christmas. Orphaned kids would have to wait until they were mothers or fathers and had their own family Christmas.

Chapter 9

Fears and Tears

When you're between five and seven years old and living in an orphanage, you share a bedroom with twenty-five other boys. There's usually a lot of crying and tears shed at night because this is the age when young boys are brought to the orphanage because of family troubles or one of the parents has an alcohol problem. Little kids are missing their mommies and daddies and have a hard time adjusting to their new environment.

Young children also get scared a lot when the weather changes and there's thunder and lightning and no parent to comfort them. Some boys climb into their friend's bed next to them, but eventually the matrons come to calm the child.

I was a lucky orphan who came to live in this home at the age of three. So did six other boys and girls whom I met there. We had no fears, not like the older kids, who had many fears.

One fall, the farm manager, Mr. Honeywell, had a group of older boys burning weeds in the irrigation ditches that had become overgrown during the summer months. Stanley, whom we called "Steamer," and his twin brother, Sterling, had also come to the orphanage at age three, just like me. We were seven years old when Steamer and I began grabbing small handfuls of weeds. Then we would twist them together into a long shaft. We watched the older boys do this as they walked backwards in the bottom of the irrigation ditch. They would torch the dried, brown weeds in the bottom of the ditch, and the fire would spread up the sides of the wall of the ditch and burn the dried weeds. Another group of boys with hoses and shovels

129

would follow the first group. They'd extinguish the burning embers, and wouldn't let the fire jump across the road.

Steamer and I had matches, and we would go 100 to 200 feet ahead of the boys who were lighting the weeds. We would light the twisted shaft of weeds, and then we would set fire to the weeds. The weeds in the ditch would burn to the top of the one-foot high, irrigation ditch.

Steamer got the idea to take some taller grass and ring it together. Then he would light the tip of it on fire, and it would make a good torch. The idea was that we could burn more weeds in the ditch, as we walked down through the alfalfa field. As we were burning the ditch, we ended up behind the bus barn. I got the idea to take out a big, five-gallon Folgers red coffee can, which was sitting alongside the incinerator in the garbage behind the kitchen.

I told Steamer to stuff it full of weeds and light the weeds with the fire in the ditch, because we had run out of matches. We could carry the can of fire across the field to get over to the irrigation ditch in the cornfield.

As we carried the coffee can with the weeds that were on fire, the coffee can became hot on the bottom as we got halfway to the cornfield. We now began to run because the can was really getting hot. I told Steamer to take his long-sleeved shirt and grab the side of the can with his shirt sleeve, so he wouldn't get burned. I already had my shirt sleeve hooked onto the can. We got within five feet of the cornfield, when the can became too hot to hold. We dropped it into the already-picked cornfield. All the dried, brown, corn stocks were lying on the ground, which immediately caught fire around the can.

We started to stomp out the fire the best we could with our lace-up farmer shoes, but the Nebraska winds, which blew strong every day, whisked the fire away from us into a bigger circle of flames.

Steamer hollered, "Jimmy, take your coat off and start beating the fire."

By this time, our coats were of no use. The fire was spreading south throughout the cornfield as the winds came from the north. Steamer and I ran towards the home. Luckily, no one was watching us. As we approached the playroom door, everybody was coming out of the basement stairs to see you what was going on because of the giant billowing clouds of smoke coming from the cornfields. We slowly walked through the crowd, down the stairs, and into the playroom. We looked at each other, and neither of us had eyebrows. We had black soot on both our hands, and blisters on all the tips of our fingers, where we had held onto the can as long as we could.

We were the only ones in the playroom, so I said, "We can't tell anyone that it was us. If anyone asks us what we were doing out in the cornfield, we'll just tell them we didn't see any fire when we were out there."

We hurried down the hall to the washroom to clean our hands and faces to get rid of the evidence. We then went back down the hall, and went outside where everyone was standing watching the billowing smoke as it spread across the whole field of corn. Everybody started questioning how the cornfield had caught on fire.

To answer that question, we just shrugged our shoulders and said, "We don't know how the cornfield fire got started, but we saw some of the boys burning irrigation ditches when we were down there."

Steamer and I climbed up the stairs to the second floor, and saw that the whole cornfield was on fire. The farmhands had gotten the gray Ford tractor and hooked up the disk behind the tractor. We could see them going back and forth at the end of the field trying to make a fire break, so the fire wouldn't burn the neighbor's cornfield. We began hearing sirens and bells from the town's fire trucks, which were fast approaching. Stanley and I never did tell anyone how that fire started. It burnt 150 acres of corn and one of the haystacks in the alfalfa field. The fear of someone finding out kept us up for a couple of nights, because our beds were next to each other in the West Room.

As you grow up in an orphanage, there are certain rules among boys to protect each other. One of the first things you learn when new boys and girls show up for the first time is that you would never ask a boy about his family. From personal experience, you know that this is a very sore spot for a young boy coming to live at the orphanage with a large group of boys. You never talk about their mother or their father because in many instances, one or the other is dead or a drunk. The boy who comes into the home with a lot of bruises or fears will never be talked about to anyone. Some children come with hate in their hearts, because of the treatment or family situation that made them devise self-survival methods to protect their emotional core. It would sometimes take these kids six months to a year before they would get involved with those of us kids who were already in the orphanage.

The staff arranges for the new kid to follow an older boy around for a couple of days. It's our duty to show them the school, where they will sleep, and how to conform to the daily routine. By doing this, the older boy starts to find out what things bother the kid, how he reacts to authority, and how he is conforming to the process of living with a lot of boys and girls.

The older boys taught me another rule when I was six or seven years old—never tell the truth to an authority figure who asks questions, such as, "Who was the person who committed the crime?" The rule was always to look down at the ground. The authorities would know if you were telling the truth or lying by watching your eyes and facial expressions. They told me to restrict my answers to yes or no, or otherwise not to volunteer any information. Under no circumstances was I to give them the name of the person in the wrong. If the older boys found out that I had given out information to the authorities, they would label me as a tattletale or a squealer. I was told that I wouldn't have too many friends among my peers after that. Besides, the older boys would either give you all the rough chores out in the fields or down at the barn. Up in the big house, you would be given assigned chores there, because the staff could watch you if you were one to be picked on as a tattletale.

A boy learned never to cry when he wanted to get something from somebody. Orphaned boys didn't cry, because it showed that you were weak. Crying too many times would again put you in a position where you wouldn't have too many friends. If you were a cry baby, you'd be back in the pecking order, and some of the big boys would pick on you, just to get you to cry.

During the spring of 1948, I was eight years old, and had been assigned to the brooder house crew. There were two brooder houses full of 200 to 300 baby chicks. Each house had five to six big tables with heat lamps over each table that glowed day and night. The staff would place the eggs upon soft straw. A calendar behind the front door is where we marked off how many days the eggs had been under the hot lamps. This also indicated how many days remained before hatching time. When the baby chicks would hatch, one of our jobs was to take the little baby chicks from the hatching table and place them on the growing table.

The older boys taught me how to pick up a newly hatched baby chick. I had to cup my hands together and surround the baby chick with each hand. Then I would lace my fingers together forming a hand cup with the baby chick's feet sticking out at the bottom of my cupped hands.

It was a surprising feeling in my hands when I picked up my first baby chick from the hatching table. Being eight years old and getting to hold a new life in my two hands that had just hatched minutes ago, was a feeling that I'd never experienced. The small yellow fluff peeped for the first time in its little life and I was carrying the chick to the growing table.

Our job was to keep the feeders and water jars full because there were fifty to one hundred baby checks on each table. Sometimes, if we noticed one of the baby chicks was not drinking water, we had to pick up the baby chick and dip its beak in the water one or two times. Then the chick would know where it had to go to get water. All day long, the chicks would just eat, drink, and peep. There were so many chicks on each table. Some chicks would squat to get some rest, and other chicks would walk right over the top of them. Feeding and caring for those chicks was a chore. Once they got to a certain age, then we could transfer the chicks into a chicken coop.

Approaching the brooder house, we could hear the baby chicks peeping seventy-five feet away from the front door. It was so noisy that we had to shout to get anyone to hear what we had to say. Once inside the brooder house, the ammonia smell from the manure would make our eyes water. The smell would also burn the inside of our nostrils until we got used to it.

One of the jobs I had was to look after the baby chicks that had gotten picked on by the other chicks. There always seemed to be four or five chicks to each table that were the runts. One or two baby chicks would start pecking the fluff off the runt's head and would try to keep him away from the feeder. The other chicks soon followed and then they, too, began pecking on the same chick. I had to watch the runts carefully, otherwise they'd have no fuzz left on their backs or heads and the other chicks would push them away from getting food and water.

As a boy in the orphanage, if you showed **any** weakness when you were among the older boys, you would become an outcast or a runt. There was a pecking order among the children and we would find this out when we were being chosen for a baseball or football lineup to play the game. I was one of the last players to be picked, since I was small and couldn't hit the ball.

One fear that Bobby Broberg and I had was being at the mercy of a bully named Edgar Smith. He had the name of "Mustard." He was ten years old, talked tough, and always picked on the smaller boys.

The story is that Edgar stole a big forty-eight ounce jar of mustard from the kitchen one afternoon. Taking the jar, he ran out to the garden and climbed into the dug-out cave the older boys had made several years earlier. He would eat the whole jar of mustard by himself. He didn't show up for dinner that night, and the staff found him in the cave with a severe bellyache. He ended up in bed for three days, and that is how he got the name of "Mustard."

For two years, he was a bully and was always picking on Bobby and myself. He would usually catch Bobby or me alone in the hallways. He would slug us on the arm or try to snap an elbow to our chest, trying to get us to fight him. When I saw him coming down the hall, I would turn and run the other way. Sometimes he would chase me. When he caught me, he would grab the front of my shirt and pull my face in front of his face.

Then he'd say, "Come on! I dare you to hit me! I dare you! Come on, hit me."

I knew enough not to say a word. Then he'd shove me backwards or push me hard up against the wall. Finally he would stomp off down the hall when I wouldn't fight him.

Just to show us how tough he could be to us, whenever Bobby or I were outdoors, he would throw clods or rocks at us, as we played on the playground. He would sometimes try to peg us down in the playroom with his orange or apple that he got for mid-afternoon snack. Once he did that, he would take our snack from us.

In the spring of 1950, I had just turned ten years old. I was in a group of four boys playing near the gas pump. The gas pump was an old-fashioned pump with a see-through glass cylinder on top of the pump. It had a long metal handle that you had to push back and forth to bring the gas into the glass cylinder on top of the pump. The older boys used the gasoline for farming with the tractors and pickup truck.

Someone mentioned that gasoline would float on water, because the irrigation ditch with water in it went right by the gasoline pump. The irrigation ditch brought water from the irrigation well located on the other side of the alfalfa field. The ditch ran down through the alfalfa field, close to the gas pump and into the cornfield behind the farm manager's house.

"Moses," the boy who pumped one gallon of gas in the glass cylinder, dared us to drain the gasoline on the water. We called him Moses because he had polio as an infant, and now he had to wear a back brace every day because of his severe scoliosis, which made him shorter than most of us who were the same age. He had a hard time keeping up with the other boys during physical activities. One of the boys took the nozzle off the pump and placed it above the running water. He squeezed the nozzle and let some gasoline go into the water in the irrigation ditch. Then one of the boys threw a match on top of the water, which lit up the gasoline with a whoosh sound. The flame traveled down about fifty feet before the flame disappeared. What a discovery for all of us to see such an amazing feat.

I awoke one morning when I was eleven years old and found that my bed was wet. I got out of bed as fast as I could. I removed my wet pajamas and quickly stuffed them under my pillow. When I went to bed that night, I didn't put on my slightly wet pajama bottoms. I just wore my pajama tops and underwear. I climbed into my bed as fast as I could, hoping none of my bedmates would see me in my underclothes or smell the pee smell. I climbed under my blanket and bedspread, with the top sheet under me. I found a dry spot on the outside of the wet spot, and slid my pajamas out from under my pillow onto the dry part of the bed. The next night, my pajamas had dried and I hurried to hang them in my locker the next day without anyone seeing me. The next night the sheets had become dry because of my body heat the night before. Becoming known as a bed-wetter was a fear of mine from that day forward.

When you live in an orphanage, you fear being labeled as a bed-wetter because the staff would put a rubber sheet underneath your regular sheets. Having to change sheets every morning is another concern, along with a shower before going down for breakfast. This was a definite fear for a young, eleven-year-old boy.

Another sign of fear is that every so often, an older boy would try to run away from the home. The Union Pacific railroad tracks, which ran north and south of the small towns, were only about a quarter-mile east of the home. Some boys would attempt to jump the train, and try to get back home to where they had come from. Some tried to hitchhike, but the highway patrol usually picked them up and brought them back on the same day.

When a kid didn't show up to eat lunch or dinner, the staff became concerned about the boy and his safety. The staff would question the kid's friends or other kids who sat at the runaway's dinner table. The staff tried to find out the last time someone had seen the runaway. Once the staff knew that the boy had truly run away, and that he wasn't just hiding, the superintendent would call the highway patrol and ask them to be on the lookout. One boy, Hank Pool, was gone for three days, but they finally found him hitchhiking in North Platte, which was approximately 150 miles away from the home.

One of my best friends at the orphanage was Bobby Broberg. Bobby came to the home when we were both eight years old. He came with three brothers who were older and his little brother, Bert, who was five years old. In the afternoon after school, he and I became cowboy friends. Every day we would dress up like cowboys—he was Roy Rogers and I was Lash La Rue. We would capture all the bad guys every day. On Saturday afternoon, while we were standing against the wooden fence with our backs to the fence, we had one foot propped up against the bottom board—the posture of a true cowboy. We promised each other that when we grew up and got out of the orphanage we would own a ranch of cattle together. We decided we would have hired hands and our own horses with beautiful saddles. Then we would become true cowboys. We talked about this many days as we built our dream together.

We became each other's brother to the point that we took a pocketknife, sliced open our middle fingers, and drew blood. We then touched our fingers to each other's finger and promised that we would be brothers forever. At the age of ten, his aunt came to take him back home to Chadron, Nebraska. Again, I had a lot of silent crying with tears rolling into my ears for many nights before I would drift off to sleep.

To find a person who you really care for to the point of giving them everything that you have in your heart, is a hard person to find. The relationship of brothers and sisters is a special place to be with your heart.

Chapter 10

Summer Time

I was the most happy and excited during two holidays every year while I lived at the orphanage. One was summer vacation when I would spend two months with Papa. The other holiday was Christmas and he would take me home for two weeks.

After the end of classes at the orphanage, my grandpa would pick me up and take me to his house. Then I would spent most of the summer living with Aunt Thelma and Uncle Frank. Papa would drive out to their farm to see me and help with different projects that needed to be done.

One of the joys of arriving at Papa's house was to see my dog, Nicky, who was waiting for me at the door.

Papa started to take care of Nicky when he had to take me to the orphanage when I was three years old. My dog, Nicky, was a black dog, and he was as tall as my waist when I was five years old. Nicky had a lot of terrier in him, but he was a Heinz 57 breed.

Every time I came to Papa's for the holidays, I would climb off the front seat of his car and run into the house looking for Nicky. He would be at the front door waiting for me to come into the house. He would come running when he heard me call him. He would run straight at me, and jump up, as if wanting me to catch him. Of course, I was too small, and he excitedly knocked me to the floor and began licking my face. His tail would swoosh back and forth as fast as it could go. I would wrap my arms around his body while lying on the floor. Then he'd wiggle out of my arms and run as fast as he could towards the front screen door. He'd hit the screen door with his forehead, and with his charging-forward force, the screen door would spring open.

He was so happy to see me that he would run circles around the outside of the house, two or three times. Then he'd run to the back screen door, and with his paws, he'd pop the door open. He'd come running inside full speed, and would stop right in front of me. Then he'd growl and grab the bottom of my jeans with his teeth. He'd start shaking my leg back and forth with a jerking motion as if he had caught a rat. He shook me so violently that I began laughing uncontrollably. Again, I fell down on the linoleum living room floor.

At that moment, he jumped on me and licked my face again. Then he'd run towards the front screen door and start the procedure all over again. To get Nicky to stop, I pulled out one of the dining room chairs as he circled the house. I stood on the chair and put my arm above my head while holding a dog treat that Papa had handed me in the time it took Nicky to run around the house. Suddenly Nicky came in the house at full speed, sprung up from the floor, and took the treat out of my hand. Because he was a powerful dog, he jumped at least seven feet high to get the treat out of my hand.

He was a fighter and attacked any larger dogs in the neighborhood. Every so often, he would come home, scoot underneath the bed, and stay there for two to three days and nights, licking his wounds. Most of the time he won the fights that he had participated in. He hung around me all those summer days and holidays. He loved me. Nicky was my kind of dog.

Papa had been living alone since 1933 after his wife died and all his children had moved out of town. He still lived in the house that he bought close to town for my mother. He had covered his little three-room house with brown, brick tarpaper. All the walls in the house were made out of tongue and groove cedarwood and were stained dark brown. The kitchen was small and compact, and only one person could stand in the kitchen to prepare meals. The wooden icebox was located on the back porch because it wouldn't fit into the kitchen area. The only furniture in the living room and dining room area was Papa's big brown leather chair, which was next to the console radio with the big round dials.

The eating area had four dark wooden dining chairs surrounding an oblong table. It was covered with a flowered oilcloth, and the table was located at the far end of the room, pushed against the kitchen wall. There was a bookcase next to the eating area window, which faced the front street. The four-tiered wooden bookcase held books, a few recent family pictures, and two old worn decks of playing cards for solitaire. A bedroom with a double bed and a goose down mattress was in the next room. In the opening between the living room and bedroom was a big brown gas heated stove, which warmed us during the winter.

The bedroom faced the backyard and had open window shelving for his African violets and other special houseplants he liked to grow. The dresser was on the wall between the bathroom and his small closet at the east end of the bedroom. He had added a large screened-in porch with storm windows on the kitchen side of the house.

His garage was an interesting place for a small boy who was five years old. It had a dirt floor and the front part of his '49 green Ford stuck through a hole that was cut out of the side of his workshop. He had placed a large canvas awning there to cover the hole in the wall. When he parked his car there, the front bumper and headlights would push the canvas into the workshop. That maneuver would allow him to close the doors to his garage.

In big, three-foot tall bins on either side of the garage, Papa saved many things that were important to him fifteen to twenty years ago. At the rear of his garage, he added a work shed that was thirty feet by fifty feet. He had taken his harness shop equipment that was not included in the sale of the shop, and moved it into the space behind the garage. This was another great place for a young boy to explore and learn a lot of how-to's from a seventy-eight-year-old man. The smell of leather mixed with dust and dirt reminded me of his shop downtown.

Papa showed me how to make belts, leather vests, and a rawhide billfold. He taught me how to take his stamping tool, and tap it with a special hammer to put designs on the leather. I also learned how to cut special designs with many of his specialized cutting tools. He showed me how to lace leather around the outside of billfolds and belts. He had drawers full of buckles, rivets, snaps, and various types of belt buckles and tips. There were rolls of different types of cowhide, sheepskin, and cutting tools with scrapers. What a great place to spend a lot of time and let your mind expand.

I spent a lot of time in his shop because he had an old six-foot-tall hand-crank music box that was made out of dark oak wood. It had a big curved glass door. It played big tin, twenty-four-inch metal records. On the bottom of this music cabinet was a metal rack that held twelve records at a time. One record would play in the music box for two to three minutes and then the record would drop into the rack with the next record moving forward; then it came up and out of the rack to continue playing the next record. The music box would wind down, and I would have to turn the crank on the side of the big box to get it to continue playing.

Underneath the player, Papa had a big pile of metal records with different tunes. He had this big black music machine in his harness shop when he was working. The front of the music box was round and glass enclosed, which read, "Brown's Harness Shop." A person could see the records turning as the punched-out triangle spikes plinked out a tune on the metal combs behind the metal disc.

Summertime at Papa's house was when he introduced me to the rest of my family. Dwight and Alfreda had lived in Lexington all their lives while raising a family. The summer when I was five years old marked the first time that I had stayed at Papa's for two weeks. He then took me over to Dwight and Alfreda's to stay with them and their two girls for two weeks. I had never stayed in a house with two girls; this was very strange for me. Julie, the oldest by one year, was always trying to be the mother to Arlene, her sister, who was the same age as I. The three of us were always playing house or hopscotch. Sometimes we would lie on the floor and color in coloring books, of which they had plenty.

Alfreda made the greatest pancakes, and I had popcorn for the first time out of a frying skillet. The girls and I would get to make sugar cookies—strips of dough with cinnamon and sugar sprinkled on top—under Alfreda's guidance.

This was my first time to play with kids who lived in the neighborhood rather than kids in the orphanage. Playing with the neighborhood kids, I gained the knowledge of the difference between homeboys and family boys. Regarding family boys, one boy called Donnie Hickman and his friend, Larry Greenlee, lived across the street. They would always come over to Julia and Arlene's and included me in their play. They would share their toys with me, and they took turns taking me to their houses to introduce me to their mother before we began playing in their bedrooms.

Homeboys at the orphanage never liked to share toys with each other. Homeboys were always out for themselves unless you had something they wanted to play with. Then, they would include you. Their manners were very sharp and demanding when they talked among themselves.

Uncle Dwight collected old cars, so the two girls and my little cousin, Ronnie, their brother who was four years younger than I, would sit in those cars and pretend we were traveling long distances. To begin with, I would stay over at Julie and Arlene's for approximately two to three days, until I'd asked to go back to Papa's to see Nicky.

As I got older—six or seven years old—I spent more time at Julie and Arlene's house because it was only five to six blocks away from Papa's house. I could walk home every night after dinner. I soon became one of the neighborhood boys, and I learned to develop childhood summer friendships.

At the age of eight or nine, Julie and Arlene would sometimes take me to the Lexington swimming pool, which was near the icehouse on Highway 30. While swimming in that pool, I met a few boys who were very rude and pushy. They reminded me of some of the orphanage kids.

The city swimming pool was built above ground and you had to climb eight to ten stairs to get to the deck of the swimming pool. On top of the concrete deck was a long bath house on the side, away from the highway on the south side. It was open to the highway with a chain-link fence enclosure. There was a high dive at the far end of the pool, along with a small spring diving board. You could see and hear the eighteen-wheeler trucks traveling on Highway 30. On the other side of the highway was the Union Pacific Railroad with two tracks for East and West railroad traffic. Most of the trains were steam trains, which burned black coal, whose soot, along with the trucks' black diesel, landed on top of the water in the pool. The pool usually opened at noon, and the bottom of the pool was black with everything that was in the air. By later in the afternoon, when all the kids were stirring the pool water, you didn't notice the blackness of the water.

Most of the time I forgot my towel. At the end of the day, I would go into the men's dressing room looking for a towel that somebody had left on the dressing bench. There always seemed to be one or two towels hanging on hooks that had been there for days. Those towels had been used repeatedly, to the point that you could smell the mold growing in the towels. I had no other choice. Therefore, I would use those towels to wipe the water off my body because I didn't have a friend who would share his towel with me. I would go home smelling a little rancid; the stink would stay with me until I took a bath.

Taking a bath at Dwight and Alfreda's was a different experience. Alfreda would put a big white tea kettle filled with water on the stove to heat our bath water. She then would get the round metal washtub from outside, bring it into her kitchen and fill it with cold water from the faucet. Dwight's house didn't have a hot water heater in those days. She would pour the hot water into the cold-water tub, making it warm enough to get in and take a bath. Julie had to go first because she was the oldest. Arlene would be second, and used the same water, except Alfreda would pour more hot water from the stove into the tub. I would be the third one in the same bath water with more hot water poured in the washtub. We would empty the tub with a small pail after we had finished, until we could pull the tub of used dirty water out to the backyard to dump it. That was another fiasco.

During the summer when I was seven years old, Uncle Don moved to Lexington with his family and his only son, Timmy. He was three years younger than I was.

Uncle Don was a handsome man, standing close to six feet tall, and he was a very personable man. He had a dimpled chin like Kirk Douglas and two dimples showed when he smiled. He had gone to high school in Lexington, so he knew all the people's families. He worked at Rosenberg's, which was an international tractor and farm equipment store located in downtown Lexington. He was one of their top salesmen for the farm equipment.

He and Papa went together and bought a prefab build-it-yourself home that you'd choose out of a catalog. Those houses came out after the war and arrived on a railroad boxcar. They bought the prefab home after selling the basement apartment they had purchased and lived in two years before.

The next summer, at age eight, I came to live with Papa, but I would spend a couple days at Uncle Don's playing with Timmy. He again was a family boy who shared all of his great outdoor toys. He had real metal trucks, tractors, and a crane to play with in his sandbox where he and I spent most of our time. He was an only child. Therefore, I learned to play with him differently. I didn't do any roughhousing with him or take his toys away from him because he would begin to pout and cry.

When I was eight, Papa came to get me for Christmas vacation. I was asked to stay with Aunt Thelma and her family, who were moving close to Lexington. However, at that time, they lived at Uncle Dee's farm, one mile west of Overton. It was a smaller town about thirteen miles from Lexington. Uncle Dee was Papa's younger brother. They lived in Dee's house until their property came out of escrow.

Her husband, Frank, who had worked with the Union Pacific Railroad as an engineer, had the beginnings of diabetes. His doctor suggested that he should find something less stressful to do, and he recommended that Frank change occupations. Frank sold their house in Kansas City. In exchange, they bought eighty acres of farmland south of Overton.

When I turned eight years old, Papa bought me a brand new bicycle, which he kept in his workshop for me to use during the summer. I explored the neighborhood, and I'd ride my bike close to the street corner and back. I expanded my block by staying on the sidewalk and riding completely around the block. Next door to Papa's house was Huff's grocery store. This was a neighborhood store where people could pick up little things that they'd run out of while cooking. The Huff's house was used to create their store. They tore out their living room to add on a big room for their small grocery store. They put in two coolers with shelving for needed canned goods. They also sold candy and ice cream as treats for the neighborhood kids.

Across the street on the northeast corner was a huge brown house with yellow trim. Adjacent to the house was a big red barn, which had a few animals in it. Cy Haggardon and his wife lived there. Mrs. Haggardon grew many types of flowers, and she always bought flower and garden seeds from me when I cased the neighborhood for sales. She and Papa got along real well for Papa's yard was full of flowers all summer long.

A lot of my summer vacations with Papa involved us spending time with Frank and Thelma on their farm. The farm was located four miles south of Overton, whose township had a population of less than 400. Lexington's population was about 4,000 and that town was thirteen miles west of Overton. Thelma and Frank had a son named Terry, who was six years older than I was. His sister, Jean Dell, had married and moved to Texas before Thelma and Frank moved to the farm in Overton.

Terry was like a big brother to me. He included me in everything he did during those weeks that I stayed on the farm, which was most of the summer. When I was nine years old, Terry had gotten his driver's license. One evening he asked his father if he could use the family car to drive into Overton to see his girlfriend, Mickey. On the nights when he had permission to use the car, Terry would drive out of the driveway but he'd always turn around, and come into the house.

He'd say, "Come on, Jimmy, you're going with me."

He just couldn't leave me at home with the folks. We would go pick up Mickey and play Monopoly or visit with their high school friends. He showed me how to shoot a rifle, go duck hunting, how to catch a ball with a catcher's mitt, and other things that big brothers do for younger brothers.

Thelma would take me to church with her on Sunday, and I would go to Sunday school. One week, she had me go to Bible school at her church. I was the one who knew all the stories of the Bible because of the stories I had learned in Sunday school at the chapel in the orphanage. All the kids at Sunday school in Overton thought I was very smart, because I knew all the Bible stories word for word.

Thelma raised small chickens during the summer until they became fryer chickens. Fryer chickens were to be processed and taken into town where Thelma rented a walk-in freezer. She'd store the chickens and beef there for the winter months.

I would get to help Thelma with her chicken-cleaning day in the middle of June. Our first job was to fill up the big cooking pot with water. The pot was at least two feet deep, oblong, and had two big wooden handles at either end. The pot must have been a twenty-gallon tin tub because it took two burners to heat the water up after four hours. This huge tin tub, full of water, sat on the outside propane gas stove. Papa would drive out to help Thelma on that day. The job that Terry and I had was to pull the pinfeathers out of the chickens and singe the chickens over the open burner. Papa would gut the chickens and Thelma would wrap them in white freezer paper. We would process between fifty and sixty chickens that day.

Twice during the summer, Papa would drive out on the days that Frank would want to stack hay, and they would build one or two big haystacks. Papa would drive the pickup truck backwards; a cable from the stacker to the front bumper of the truck lifted the stacker's front forks. This action would lift the stacker up with a load of hay, and it would fall on top of the haystack. Uncle Frank used the tractor to pull the stacker from the barnyard to the haystack, placing it out in the alfalfa field. The stacker would throw the hay onto the top of a haystack, and the pile grew taller and taller with each load of hay.

When I was young, my job was to help Thelma and the other ladies prepare lunch for all the farmhands, who came to help Frank and Terry stack hay. My job also was to take water out to the haystack, along with snacks for the farmhands, during their mid-morning and afternoon breaks.

Staying at Papa's house during the summer was fun. I learned many things from him over those summers and holidays. One of the things I learned about Papa was that he loved to play pinochle. Every Tuesday and Thursday evening he would go to the Odd Fellows Hall located above the Ralph Theater downtown. He and his regular friends would play pinochle until midnight on those nights. At age seven, he would give me a quarter, allowing me to go downstairs and across the street to the Majestic movie house. It cost fifteen cents for the movie and ten cents for the popcorn. I must have gone to every movie that came into town for the summer. Movies were against our religion at the orphanage and the staff told us we would go to hell if we watched movies. Therefore, I loved the movies and knew I was going to go to hell.

Almost every day during the summer, Papa would go fishing with his pals. That's where he taught me a lot of things about fishing. I learned how to bait a hook using minnows or fish worms, and I watched the red and white bobber movements and learned that I had to count to three before yanking on the line.

I learned my odd eating habits from Papa, such as putting sugar on the Romaine lettuce leaf. Then I'd roll up the leaf, and eat it with liver and onions that night for supper. He showed me how to boil three-minute eggs, and how to make pancakes with milk or water—depending upon what was in the refrigerator that morning.

The greatest thing to eat was Papa's homemade cinnamon toast. He would sprinkle sugar and cinnamon on top of a piece of white bread that had a lot of soft yellow butter spread on the top. He would place the bread slices into the broiler of his little stove. Now I know where my mama learned the trick of making cinnamon toast. On some mornings, I would eat seven pieces of this delicious toast with a glass of milk. Then he would take me out to his workshop, and help me find my fishing pole, which was a long cane pole with a bobber attached to the line. Next, I'd climb in the car and we'd go fishing with his friend, Jesse.

Being out on the farm, Terry and I had many spots to place, throw, or tie the firecrackers—with the concept of trying to destroy things. Once, we dropped an M1 in a bucket of water. After the explosion, the bucket was completely bent out of shape. Another great sport we enjoyed was blowing tin cans ten to twelve feet into the air, while trying to catch the can as it fell to the ground. One day Terry drove to the local sand pit out by the Platte River. Terry taped an M1 to a big rock, lit the M1, and it sank in the water. Small bubbles rose to the surface of the water. After thirty seconds, water would shoot straight up in the air. We'd wait for one or two minutes, and then we'd start counting how many fish would come to the top—either stunned or dead.

Terry found a lead pipe approximately a foot and a half long. He plugged up one end with mud and a smaller pipe cap. He then would drop a two-inch red firecracker into the open end of the pipe. Next, he'd place a Chinese checker marble, which came out of his game set, on top of the lit firecracker. The thing would go off, but we could never find the marble. We were shooting this pipe off into the front yard of the farmhouse. Terry got an idea and loaded the pipe up, and aimed it with the marble to bounce off the screen door. He would stand back in the yard with his baseball glove and catch the marble as it bounced off the screen door. My big job was to hold the pipe as it went off. He lit the firecracker, and I dropped the marble into the pipe. I took careful aim, with the pipe aiming at a slant, and pointed it at the front screen door. The firecracker went off. The marble put a hole through the screen door, the front door, and then it shot across the bedroom. The marble was buried two inches deep in the plaster wall.

Terry and I went into the house to find the marble after we came out of shock. We never thought that the marble would go through the screen door and the wooden front door. We looked at the hole in the door, and then turned and saw that the marble was embedded in the wall, which was only two inches away from Aunt Thelma's big, round, beautiful mirror above her vanity table. To say the least, we didn't shoot marbles anymore.

At the end of that summer, I stayed at Papa's house, and got to explore his garage, which was a goldmine for a young boy of ten years old. I found many interesting things that he had stored in his garage. The first thing I discovered was a pinball machine without legs, and a baking oven that was used over a fire pit while camping. It took me half of a day to pull everything out of the bin on one side of the garage. I also found an old army tent, along with a ham radio, and some old camping equipment.

The next door neighbor boy, Paul, and I found a pile of old lumber alongside Papa's garage. We started moving the 2 x 4's up and into the big Mulberry tree between Paul's granddad's storage shed and Papa's garage. After we built the base, then we began to build a flat platform with the plank wood we had found. We then could hang the tent above the platform. We made a rope ladder to get up in the tree tent. We could hoist up the ladder to keep other people out of our army headquarters. We also used an old radio with earphones, which he and I had found in the garage bin. We had a lot of fun with our Army maneuvers the whole summer.

One of the best things about staying at Papa's house when I was ten years old was to crawl into Papa's lap and ask him questions. In the orphanage, I never had any skin contact with any adults, except maybe at bath time when the matron used Jergen's lotion on my chapped hands and elbows. Papa had a lot of thin white hair, and sometimes he wouldn't shave for two or three days. Then he'd have stubby white hair all over his face. He wore gold, round-rimmed glasses, and he smoked unfiltered cigarettes. There was no such thing as a filtered cigarette when I was a young boy. Papa sometimes would send me over to Huff's store to buy a carton of Camels cigarettes for him.

I would play with his stubby chin, and all of a sudden, he would growl, shake his head from side to side, and then he'd open his mouth as if he was going to bite me. I would jump with fright.

He would laugh, and say, "I got you."

Then he would be quiet, and it would start all over again. After two or three of these attacks, I would ask Papa about his life when we was growing up.

I remember asking him, "What was your first job, Papa?"

He told me that he did harvesting with a great big steam tractor, and his job was to load the wheat straw into the shifter. This shifter would shake the wheat kernels off the shaft. The wheat kernel was used for making flour, and the rest was sold to the granaries in town. The straw shafts then were stored in the barn for use during the winter.

I then asked him about his next job, and he would talk to me with words that formed a picture in my mind of the whole scene. He was a great storyteller.

He told me about his interview with Buffalo Bill. This interview started when Buffalo Bill traveled with his Wild West Show. The show came to Lexington one summer on its way to North Platte. Papa was walking down the street in Lexington, when all of a sudden a big white stallion horse with two riders astride rode down the middle of the street. Suddenly, the horse turned and went through the swinging doors of the bar. Papa ran into the bar to see what was going on. The man who rode the horse wore a white, ten-gallon Stetson hat over his flowing white hair that hung down to his shoulders. He leapt off his horse and stood up on the bar. He wore a black striped suit with a red dotted bowtie and a black bowler hat. He took off his bowler hat, reached inside it, and pulled out a brown rawhide sack.

He then shouted as he held the sack of coins above his head, "The drinks are on Bill Cody."

As he turned the sack of coins upside down, the gold coins bounced off the top of the bar. The rider was Bill Cody himself, dressed in a white buckskin coat with streamers down his arms and across his back. He also donned fancy white gloves with leather streamers.

He lifted his white Stetson ten-gallon hat, and said, "Come see me tonight at our first show. I will have a shootout with Annie Oakley."

He turned his horse toward the door, and he leaned back, while pulling hard on the reins. He made his horse's front legs rise up into the air, kicking. The white stallion came back down with a heavy thud on the wooden floor. Then Wild Bill walked his horse out into the street.

Papa continued with his story and told me that he went out to the showground and was able to set up an interview with Buffalo Bill for noon the next day regarding a job with his Wild West show.

On that next day, at noon, Papa stepped into Wild Bill's room at the downtown Cornland Hotel, where Buffalo Bill was staying for the duration of the show. After Buffalo Bill shook hands with Papa, he sat down behind a big oak desk in his room. Papa sat in the big printed wing-backed chair on the other side of the desk. He could smell the alcohol, sweat, and the tobacco chew which was at the corner of Buffalo Bill's mouth.

Buffalo Bill started asking Papa several questions. As Papa answered each question with a long dissertation, Bill Cody closed his eyes. His chin dropped to his chest, and he either fell asleep or passed out—probably because of the alcohol that he had consumed that morning. Papa stopped talking in mid-sentence. He slowly stood up, and very quietly walked out of the room.

Papa said, "I would never work for a drunk."

Then Papa, with a slight grin, said, "I did get a free pass to the Wild West Show, though."

In those days, we didn't have television, so Papa would sit in his favorite chair and listen to the radio shows. I either climbed into his lap or laid down on the floor next to his chair with Nicky, in front of the console radio. We loved to listen to "Amos and Andy," "Fibber McGee and Molly," and "The Shadow." Those radio programs came on every night. Papa would get us a glass of milk and saltine crackers before we would get ready for bed.

I learned a lot about living with those three families through the summer months. I learned how most families functioned. When I went into somebody's house and stayed for one or two weeks, I would have to be very quiet and mind my manners. I observed the interactions of the children with their parents, because I quickly learned my guidelines to being a good, behaved boy. Otherwise, I would have been a mischievous nuisance of a boy who didn't follow the rules of the household.

Secondly, when I was invited to someone's home for dinner, I was told that I should never ask for second helpings. I didn't want to offend the mother by asking for more food because that might be all the food they had for that day. Some families didn't have enough money for food for the next day.

I always waited until somebody asked, "Jimmy, would you like to have more of the leftover food?"

Another thing I learned was never to tell the mother of the family that I didn't like a particular food she was serving. I ate what was on my plate and all of it—even if I didn't like it.

After six years of summer vacations, I stayed in those family's homes and got to know them very well. I found out one important fact. I know that I was welcomed into all their families, but none of the adults ever picked me up, or put their arms around my neck, and said, "Jimmy, I love you."

I knew deep in my heart that Aunt Thelma loved me like her own child. She couldn't say that she loved me, because of her commitment to Jean Dell and Terry. Her husband, Frank, also didn't want to hear her say those words, for he wanted her for himself.

Aunt Thelma was the closest person that I had as a mother. She looked after me by keeping my clothes clean, my belly full, and she gave me pocket change to spend on Saturday nights in Overton. She even sewed patterned, short-sleeved shirts for me that were made out of the five-pound flour bags, which she bought on Saturday night in Overton.

On one summer day when I was around eleven years old, Aunt Thelma asked me, "Jimmy, would you write me a letter once in awhile when you grow up and move away from here?"

At that time, I was sitting alone in the car with her while we were waiting for someone to come out of a store. I wondered why she had asked me that question.

I replied, "Of course, I will. Why did you ask me such a question?"

She said, "Terry is now away at college, and I never hear from him except when he comes home for vacations."

She looked directly at me, and then continued, "My heart misses him, and I worry about different things, like what he's doing or isn't doing. I know he is a boy and he is busy trying to find his life, but a phone call or a little note would make me feel better, especially at night."

After a short pause, she said, "When you grow up, you, too, will move away and I will never hear from you again."

I looked directly into her eyes, and I said, "I promise I will always keep in touch with you, no matter where I live."

On that day, I knew she was trying to tell me she loved me as much as she loved Terry. She couldn't say those words, "I love you," even though she was my mother's oldest sister. She took care of me as best as she could.

Chapter 11

The Last Trip

After Grandpa picked me up from the orphanage to take me to Lexington for summer vacation, he told me we were going to a local park to have a potluck picnic with everyone in the Brown family. Papa's family included all three of his children and their families who lived in and around Lexington. He also had a sister and two brothers who lived near Omaha. There were distant cousins living in the hills of Lexington, who would drive to Lexington for this picnic too.

Someone would bring the meat, and then other families would bring salads and vegetables like corn on the cob, cooked green beans, and other garden dishes. Almost everybody had a garden in their backyard to help them get through the summer months. Of course, each family brought their own special dessert to share.

All the young kids got together to play on the park equipment, while the young adults played softball, with each family choosing sides. The elderly members of the family and the ladies would sit underneath the shade trees on picnic benches or on individual folding chairs, talking about family tales. The key to picnics was that everybody had to see whose kids were associated with each family.

Since I had two families—the orphanage kids versus the family kids—at the age of ten or eleven, I began to notice things that most family children would take for granted. I would watch the interactions between children and their parents and relatives.

The young kids got to sit on somebody's lap, and the adults would wrap their arms around the young kids for long periods. Some of the girls and little kids had to sit on two or three different laps throughout the day.

Orphan kids never got to sit on anyone's lap, unless it was their older sister or brother's lap, while attending Sunday school or church.

With a child on their lap, the adult would lean their face up alongside the child's head while they were just sitting and listening to family conversations. This was a sign of true love from an older adult or mother, who cares. Hands brushing up and down the child's arms were another sign. Fingers running through the children's hair, while sitting on their grandparents' or aunts' laps was another sign of caring.

A small family child who got an "ouch" or a scrape while playing at the picnic received a concerned adult's care to pick them up. They also received kisses, and the adult would make a fuss over their problems until they quit crying.

One time, as an orphan kid, I got a severe cut one afternoon while playing in the bus barn at the orphanage. I thought I couldn't walk. One of the older boys picked me up and carried me upstairs to the matron. By the time the older kid picked me up, I had stopped crying, although tears kept rolling down the sides of my face because of the pain. When the older boy placed me on the emergency table located upstairs in the dormitory, I started whimpering, because of the pain the matron bestowed upon me. She was cleaning out the wound using a square scrubbing gauze saturated with hydrogen peroxide. The older boy and a couple of others were standing by watching the procedure. I tried to show the boys that I was brave. The next thing the matron did was to get out the iodine. She put it on a clean square gauze and covered the wound with a gauze wrap. I couldn't help but cry. The boys suddenly turned to go downstairs, and they continued their play where they had left off. I remained lying on the matron's table for a while until I wanted to get up. I limped to the chair located in the hallway of the dormitory to sit down.

When you had an older sister or brother, the matron would send someone to find them so they could console you. The matron was too busy with other chores to pay much attention to you. Since I didn't have a sibling who lived at the orphanage with me, I just went downstairs and began playing again.

A family boy sometimes got his hair ruffled up by the uncle or dad who thought he had done something that pleased them. Orphan kids' hair never was ruffled up since there were no adults who would ruffle up your hair, because you did something to please them.

The closest thing to being in someone's lap, as an orphan boy, was when I was placed across an adult's lap to receive a whipping for doing something I shouldn't have done.

While coming and going to family functions, I noticed the smell of perfume when I was sitting in a car with a lady. Orphaned kids never got to sit in the car, let alone smell a lady who wore perfume.

During Christmas vacation, I had asked Aunt Thelma if I could bring another boy home with me at Easter time. At the age of eleven, Easter was coming, and I told Stanley Steamer that I would like to have him come with me to Aunt Thelma's place for Easter vacation. Stanley, with his brother, Sterling, had never gone anywhere, since they entered the orphanage at age three. Stanley had always been a bed wetter ever since we were three years old. Me, along with Stanley, and his twin brother, Sterling, all arrived at the orphanage when we were three years old.

Aunt Thelma told me she had a new job in Holdrege cracking eggs for a cake company. She would get on a bus in Overton at five in the morning, with eight to ten other ladies riding over to Holdrege. They had to arrive at work by 7:00 a.m. every day of the week. I thought she might take Stanley and I home with her for Easter, but I couldn't risk taking him if he was going to wet the bed.

I got a notebook out, and told Stanley I would keep track of the days he wet the bed. I also wanted to know the days when he didn't wet the bed.

His bed was next to mine, and every night before we crawled into bed, I would say to Stanley, "Please go to the bathroom before you climb into bed."

I would say my prayers in silence except for the end, where I would say out loud, "Please don't let Stanley wet the bed tonight. Amen."

The first week I recorded six days of no wet bed. Then an accident happened, and we had to start all over to get a perfect week. There were approximately five weeks before Easter vacation and Stanley was doing very well with not wetting the bed. Even the kids in our room started cheering when Stanley would get out of bed in the morning announcing he was dry.

Stanley was so excited about coming with me to Aunt Thelma's farm. During the third week, I wrote a letter to Aunt Thelma, and told her that I was going to bring a friend home with me for Easter. She wrote back saying that would be good if I brought a friend. She also wrote that we should meet her at the city park at five o'clock. She would make the new yellow bus wait until we got there. We could then ride home with her to Overton, with all the old ladies.

The day before Easter, Stanley was still dry that morning, and everybody cheered as he had gone forty-one days without wetting the bed. Even the matron was happy that Stanley had stopped wetting the bed. We got our clothes together that morning, and put them in one suitcase that the matron had given us to use for our trip. We went down to the barn to take care of all our pig chores, had breakfast, and went to school for the last day before Easter vacation. After school, we got our things and carried our suitcase to the superintendent's office. We stood in front of the secretary's window, which was so high up that we couldn't see her. We knew she was there because we could hear her typewriter clicking. I went to the door and knocked very hard.

She opened the door and I asked the young, pretty-faced secretary if someone would drive Stanley and I into town to meet Aunt Thelma at the park. The superintendent, hearing my request, called us into his office. He asked us to sit down and told us that we hadn't told him about Stanley and I going to Aunt Thelma's house for Easter. Therefore, he was not going to take us to town to meet Aunt Thelma. He was not interested in Stanley's achievement.

I said, "Sir, you do not understand what we accomplished."

He sat behind his desk with his arms folded in front of him. His face was round and plump, and he had very piercing eyes.

As he squinted, he said, "What do you mean, accomplished?"

I unfastened our little green tattered suitcase, reached in and took out my notebook, which was lying on top of our folded clothing. I placed it upon his desk, in the front of the inkwell. I turned the little notebook towards him so he could read it. I then stood beside him and pointed to the square that had the number of days that Stanley had not wet the bed.

I said, "I know you don't know this, but Stanley has been wetting the bed ever since he was a baby." I continued, "As you can see here," and I pointed to the last square that was heavily marked and circled four to five times, "it has been forty-one days and Stanley hasn't wet his bed."

As he stood up, he said, "That is a fine achievement but you didn't inform me of this endeavor. I will ask you to take your suitcase back upstairs, because we are not going into town."

We felt like rejected little boys whose dream had been shattered by the superintendent. Living in an orphanage, you get used to rejections, either by your playmates or the adult staff, but rejection by a superintendent who is supposed to be on your side, was a dream-shattering blow. The next day the office summoned me, because they told me I had a phone call from Aunt Thelma. I picked up the phone and listened.

Aunt Thelma said, "I had the bus waiting on the corner with a busload of ladies for half an hour yesterday evening. We began to wonder what happened to you and your friend."

I told her, "The superintendent would not take us into town to meet you." With sadness in my voice I said, "I don't know how he didn't know about our project, because all the boys, along with the matron knew about our experiment."

I continued, "I didn't know how to get a hold of you to tell you that we couldn't come. I had to stay at the orphanage."

The rest of the Easter week Stanley went on staying dry and never wet his bed ever again.

A month later school was out, and I was scheduled to go to Lexington for the summer. The matron upstairs packed everything that I owned into one big cardboard box. I had never seen such a big cardboard box. I usually took two little boxes full of two pairs of jeans with my two shirts to Papa's for the summer.

During that summer, some of the boys had to help haul this big cardboard box down to the front stairs outside, where I was to meet Papa. As I passed the front desk, the secretary came out and handed me an envelope, which was sealed.

She said to me, "Jimmy, give this to your grandpa when he comes today."

After Papa picked me up at the orphanage, we were driving to Lexington when he asked, "Jimmy, why do you have such a big box?"

I told him, "I don't know, but the secretary gave me this letter for you to read."

We got to his house, and when I went inside, I was attacked by Nicky, as always.

Now that I was eleven years old, I was much taller when I stood on the metal stool that I placed upon the dark wood dining chair. Nicky ran out the front door, circled the house, and ran back in through the back door. He performed the same routine every summer. He grabbed my pant leg and started shaking it until I had to sit down on the floor. Then he jumped on top of me, and licked my face. I knew I was home for the summer.

Papa opened the sealed envelope and read the contents, while all this action was going on in the living room. I had learned a long time ago not to ask what was in the envelope until the adult revealed what he wanted me to know.

I asked Papa, "Did I do anything wrong?"

I thought that perhaps the superintendent was upset with me over the bedwetting situation.

Papa said, "Nothing that can't be fixed."

In my mind, I thought they had sent me home for good, because of all the times I had been sent to the superintendent's office that year.

A couple of weeks later, Papa took me to Aunt Thelma's farm. I was so happy to see Terry, and he had acquired the job of driving a truck for the hay mill again this year.

A week later, Thelma asked me if I would like to go over to Dave Bolen's because David had asked if I could stay for a couple of days. Mr. Bolen and his wife were the farmers who lived across the road. I had gone over to his house the last couple of summers, and sometimes I stayed there for a couple of days. One summer he had a young niece come stay with them. They had never had children, but they seemed to enjoy their young niece, Peggy, and me. I stayed at their house for a full week, which was during the last part of the week when Peggy had come for her visit.

Dave loved to have both of us go with him to the stockyards in Kearny on Thursday afternoon. He was always buying cows or selling a cow. On the way home from the sale barn, Dave always stopped at the Dairy Queen, and he would share a banana split among the three of us.

One evening, I woke up not knowing where I was. I tried to get my bearings. I realized there was a severe thunderstorm with a lot of lightning and loud thunder. I started to get scared, not knowing where anyone was located. I headed towards the door of my bedroom. I opened the door and stepped into the hallway, only to find Peggy, who was crying and scared, standing in her doorway.

I grabbed her hand and told her, "It will be all right. Peggy, follow me."

I led her down the hallway, found the stairs, and we both went up the stairs looking for the master bedroom. Since the lightning lit up the stairs, we found our way, despite the loud thunder rumbling through the house. As we reached the door, Dave opened it as we approached.

Pointing towards the bed, he told us, "Go jump in the bed."

Just as he said that, a bright flash lit up the room from the lightning that struck a tree outside their upstairs window, and then we heard the loud, cracking noise. Peggy and I screamed. As we ran towards the bed, there was Mrs. Bolen. She lifted the covers, and we both dove into the bed, grabbing onto Mrs. Bolen as she covered us up. Just then, we heard a deep, rolling thunder sound echoing throughout the room, like the house was beginning to fall on top of us. Peggy and I had grabbed onto Mrs. Bolen's leg and we hung onto her for dear life. Dave got into bed on the other side of Mrs. Bolen.

He shouted, "Hang on. There's going to be a big one coming."

We stayed under the covers for another ten minutes with our eyes closed. As the storm passed over, it grew quieter. Mrs. Bolen told us to stay in their bed for the rest of the night. Peggy and I were safe and we finally fell asleep.

I have never been in a bed with an adult during a thunderstorm. In the orphanage, I would just have to pull the covers over my head, and I would start praying to God that the lightning would not strike the building or even my bed. It felt so nice and secure sleeping that night with the Bolen's in their bed.

Mrs. Bolen was a nice, kind lady. She also knew how to cook. She liked to have Peggy around her in the kitchen to help her cook and clean. In the mornings, I followed behind Dave to help feed the cattle, and I watched him milk the three milk cows in the barn. He showed me how to feed the many cats that were out in the barn, too. One of the little black cats became a very good friend of mine. He followed me around the yard and up to the house. He would wait on the top step at the back door for me to come out and play with him. Dave also had a horse, which he would put the saddle and bridle on, so Peggy and I could ride around the yard.

One day while Dave was out in the field and Mrs. Bolen was in the kitchen preparing a meal for lunch, I went out to the garage and climbed in their car. I pretended I was driving. I loved to sit in cars because I never had the chance to sit in a car because I lived in the orphanage. All of a sudden, Peggy opened the passenger door and poked her head inside the car.

She said, "Jimmy, what are you doing out here in the car?"

I turned to her and said, "I am pretending I'm driving to town to pick up some groceries."

She said, "You don't mind if I ride with you, do you?"

She slid into the front seat and sat very cozy close to me as I had both my hands on the steering wheel.

She wrapped her arm around my right arm, and said, "I will be your wife."

She turned the dials on the radio and played along with my pretend game.

She asked, "What kind of music do you like?" Before I could answer, she said, "You look so cute driving."

I continued my pretend drive and I was smiling because it was fun playing make-believe.

Then Peggy pulled my right hand off the steering wheel and I looked at her.

She said, "Husband, I would like to kiss you."

She touched her lips to my lips. I didn't know what to do. My eyes were wide open, and I could see her eyes were closed. It was a funny feeling. I had never kissed a girl before—not even one of my aunts—especially not on their lips—woohoo. I thought aunts were supposed to kiss you when you first saw them. Nevertheless, my aunts never did.

Peggy said, "If you were my husband, I would ask you to put your arm around my neck."

I put my arm around her neck. Then she grabbed my face and gave me a long kiss. Halfway through the kiss, I closed my eyes, which really didn't make a difference. Just then, we heard Dave on the tractor with its put-put noise that a John Deere makes, driving into the gravel yard making that crunched gravel noise. Peggy slid over to the passenger door and opened it. She ran out into the yard to meet Dave as he got off the tractor. They both went in the house for lunch. I followed a few minutes later.

Peggy and I never got out to the car again. At the end of that week, I said goodbye to Peggy, as I picked up my bag from Dave's truck when he dropped me off at Aunt Thelma's yard. Peggy turned her face towards me as I got out of the truck. She gave me a big wide smile that went straight to my heart. Then he drove Peggy to Lexington, where she lived with her family.

Thelma asked me if I had a good time over at Dave's house. I said it was great fun, and I really liked Dave and his wife, Margie. That evening, David and Margie came over to speak with Thelma about me. They told her that after this last week, Margie couldn't handle children being around all the time. Dave and his wife had lost their young son at the age of three years old from drowning in a bathtub, and Margie didn't want to open any old wounds.

I knew Dave loved me for the way he always kidded with me, and let me do farm chores with him, along with the way he talked to me. I again was disappointed, but I had learned a long time ago not to wish for anything. I just had to let things happen. Then if it didn't happen like I wanted it to, I wouldn't be so hurt and disappointed. The same thing happened when the superintendent wouldn't let Stanley go home with me for Easter. Sometimes hurts like those sear our soul. One thing is for sure; you never forget them.

Saturday evenings were a lot of fun in Overton because all the farmers who lived within ten miles would come into town. On Saturday evenings, the ladies would buy their groceries and catch up on the local gossip. The men would sit in their cars or pickup trucks and discuss what men discuss while their wives are buying groceries. Terry took me into town in his new car to pick up his girlfriend, Mickey. Then they took me to the movies and to the skating rink. That was my first experience of Overton on a Saturday night.

Overton had perhaps a population of 300 people who lived in the town. The town folks would show a movie every Saturday on the outside wall of the skating rink. One of the local farmers would put out twenty to thirty bales of straw in the vacant lot next to the skating rink wall for everyone to sit on. A big white canvas covered the side of the building, and this allowed the projected movie to be seen by everyone.

After the movie, all the kids would go to the skating rink. We rented roller skates, or as we called them—shoe skates—and we would skate around in a big circle all night long to recorded music.

I got to know a few of the kids who were in my Sunday school class that last summer. They would help me out when I fell down in the middle of the circle. I was just learning to skate with shoe skates like all the rest of the kids. Terry and Mickey would sometimes pick me up, and they would take me by the hand and pull me around the rink, so I wouldn't fall down. The skates that we had at the orphanage were metal skates that clamped onto the soles of your shoes. We had to have a skate key to tighten the skates so they would not fall off. Another thing that was different was that the wheels at the roller rink were wooden, which took me some getting used to, because they would slide to the side as

I went around the corner. Of course, as the evening progressed, every once in awhile, Mickey and Terry would come by on their skates and take me around the rink with them a couple of times.

Summertime heat got to me as I skated in the presence of forty to fifty children inside a small auditorium. We had to go outside every once in awhile to get some fresh air. There was no air-conditioning anywhere in Overton except at Holm's meat locker. Saturday nights were fun in Overton.

One day, Thelma told me that she was going to take me into Overton to introduce me to the Slager's who had seen me on Saturday night. She said they wanted to get to know me better. They were interested in having me stay with them for a week. Therefore, Thelma and I were to go over to their house for introductions. Their house was close to the high school and two doors over was a friend of mine whom I had met last year.

I packed up some of my jeans along with two shirts. Thelma and I drove to meet Mr. and Mrs. Slager. They had a nice white house with dark green trim and windows. They also had a big screened-in porch with wicker chairs and a swing.

Thelma and I walked up to the front door and Mr. Slager greeted us and escorted us into their large, well-furnished living room. We walked in and sat down on the golden three-cushion couch. After the introductions, he went over to adjust the fan in our direction. Mrs. Slager asked us if we would like something to drink. She then disappeared into the kitchen, and came back with a tray that had four glasses and a big pitcher of iced tea. Most of the conversation turned towards me.

They asked me questions like, "What do you like to eat?"

My answer was, "I like everything."

"What things do you like to do when playing?"

My answer was, "Ride my bike."

"Do you have any friends in Overton?"

My answer was, "Jerry Woodward and Tom Cogan."

Mrs. Slager said, "The Woodward's grandfather lives two houses down. Is that where I've seen you before, Jimmy?"

Of course, all my answers were answered with one or two words with my eyes cast down to the ground.

Then the question came, "Would you like to stay with us for a week?"

Through most of the conversation, I was looking down at the floor when answering their questions. Sometimes, I would shrug my shoulders and say, "I guess."

I had fun that week. We went to Kearney one evening to see a Western starring John Wayne in Technicolor. Mr. Slager drove me to Thelma's farm to pick up my bicycle. That allowed me to ride in town for the week. Mrs. Slager and I went to Lexington to shop for some clothing for me. She bought me a shirt and some slacks, and then we had lunch with a friend of hers.

At the end of the week, Thelma came over to their house to meet with Mrs. Slager and me. We again gathered in the living room. This time we had lemonade along with small cinnamon rolls that Mrs. Slager had made earlier that morning. She had found out that cinnamon rolls were one of my favorites.

Mrs. Slager said, "Mr. Slager couldn't be here today, because he got tied up with a difficult problem at work. He works at the local post office."

Then the conversation went in a new direction.

Thelma asked, "Jimmy, did you have fun this week?"

I responded, "Yes, we went to Kearney for a movie, and Mrs. Slager and I went shopping in Lexington yesterday. This is my new shirt. Do you like it?"

Thelma spoke again, "Did you enjoy the Slager's home?"

I said, "Yes, I have a room upstairs, and I got to go down the street to play with Jerry Woodward."

After more of these inquisitive questions, Mrs. Slager said, "Jimmy and I had a great time together. I learned how to play Monopoly, and I learned a lot about Junior Legion baseball."

Thelma's next conversation began, "If the Slager's make a decision, they would like you to stay here with them and go to school at Overton High, where Terry went to school."

That statement came as a surprise to me, and I wasn't ready to think about staying there.

Then Thelma said, "Frank and I will still be living on the farm where you can come and visit us whenever you like."

Mrs. Slager and I didn't respond. I was trying to grasp the first sentence about me staying there.

Thelma continued, "Papa is seventy-eight years old, and he won't be around after a couple years. Terry will be going away to college this fall, and he'll only come home on Thanksgiving and Christmas."

Thelma was talking to herself because she didn't want this to happen. She really wanted me to be hers, but I couldn't because of her husband.

Then she said, "I will come to Overton to see you in your sports events and school plays as you go through high school."

Again, I was not very talkative and I continued to stare at the floor while I answered her questions.

Then she asked, "Jimmy, do you think you would like to live here?"

There was a very long silence. Before she got to that question, tears started to form in my eyes. I didn't want tears, but my mind took over the feelings of my heart. The statements about Papa not being around in a couple years, combined with the statement of Terry going off to college were too much for me to think about at that moment.

In my mind, I was never going to see Terry again. Because of the tears that were welling up in my eyes, Mrs. Slager began wiping her eyes. This brought softhearted Aunt Thelma to tears with the silence in the room.

Finally, Thelma stood up, came over to me, and took my hand. She motioned for me to stand up.

Thelma said to Mrs. Slager, "We have to be going now. Why don't you and Mr. Slager discuss what you would like to do about Jimmy? I will call you in the next couple of days."

After that day, no one asked me if I would like to stay with the Slager's or go to school in Overton. That was the end of my adoption possibilities, which could have had a different outcome if there had been someone there who could have talked matter-of-factly and not by matters of the heart.

I thought about the situation for the next two days. I would have loved to have a mother and father like the Slager's. We did have fun. Again, I learned not to be disappointed, because I didn't wish it to be true.

During the rest of the summer, I spent my time out on the farm. Terry was very much involved in the Junior Legion baseball. Again, he took me to every practice and every game. At the beginning of the season, the coach came to me and asked if I would like to be the baseball team's batboy. Terry took me down to the store, and bought me a pair of baseball cleats. When Terry and I got home, Thelma got out her big gray Sears catalog and ordered me a baseball uniform that matched Terry's team uniform. She found a baseball cap in the catalog as well. When the cap and uniform arrived in the mailbox, she sewed the Junior Legion emblem on the front of the cap. One of the guys on the team gave me his old baseball glove.

I sat at the end of the baseball bench during every game. As soon as one of our team's batters hit the ball, I ran out to home plate and picked up the bat. Then I brought it back to the bench. I was to keep the bats stacked in order, along with the ball bag under my bench. Whenever the umpire needed a ball, I would bring the bag out to him on his signal.

Terry's Junior Legion team had won their district playoff. The team had to travel in cars 120 miles to Ogallala, for the state playoffs.

Our team had beaten three teams in the state playoffs. It was the last game for the championship with the possibilities of playing other states. The game was two to two in the top of the ninth inning. We had a man on second and third. There were two outs. Terry, the team's best hitter, was at bat. I sat on the end of the bench taking care of the bats. The batter hit a ball down the first baseline, and the ball hit the first base bag and bounced back under our bench. I jumped up and scampered behind the bench. I knew I was small enough to fit between the fence and the bench. I picked up the ball and threw it to the catcher.

Suddenly the ump yelled, as he looked over at me. He threw his arms up in the air and hollered, "OUT!"

The ball was a live ball when it hit the first base, and I didn't know what was happening. I was just helping, as always. Half the team that was sitting on the bench with me also didn't know what was happening. Nevertheless, we lost the game and the state championship that night because of a ball that I threw to the umpire. I felt very bad all the way back to Overton. That was the first game that Uncle Frank had attended that summer. I sat up front between him and Terry on the long, long ride home.

He tried to console me and whispered to me in a very low voice, "Jimmy, it is only one baseball game. There are many more games."

On the way home, it was a three-hour trip. I fell asleep soon after Uncle Frank consoled me.

Terry was a very good shortstop and he hit the ball well when he got up to bat. Lexington's team called him during the state championship and asked him to come play on their team for the rest of the summer.

July and August was when the corn seed companies hired high school kids to go out and detassel the seed cornfields that they had contracted with local farmers.

Some of the cornfields were seed cornfields that were raised and sold to the farmer for planting corn in the spring. Most of the cornfields were used for feeding the livestock, chickens, and to make flour for the markets.

Detassel crews consisted of twenty to thirty boys and girls who were tall enough to reach the top of the stalks of corn in the fields. The stocks of corn in those days grew to be six to seven feet tall.

The crews assembled in Overton early in the morning at six o'clock. Everyone would bring a lunch box, a water resistant coat, sweatshirt, and tennis shoes. Rubber bands were another item that we learned to bring to the job. They kept the cuffs of our long-sleeved shirts tight around our wrists. The purpose was to keep the pollen out of our sleeves. Sunscreen was another needed item, along with wide brim hats to keep the sun off our faces and ears.

The crews traveled to the fields in a cattle semi-truck that waited for us every morning. All the crew would climb into the back of the cattle truck. Roll call was taken by the crew chief, and then he would holler to the driver to get going after everyone was accounted for on that day. It was usually a thirty to forty-five minute ride, before we got to the cornfields. The fields in the morning were wet with dew, and some of the fields were irrigated all night. The boys and girls got out, and followed the crew chiefs that they would work under because of the assignments. Each row had one boy or girl. Each person was to take each side of the row, start walking slowly down through the field, pull every top tassel out of every stock, and then throw it to the ground. Some of the time, the field had mud that was up to our ankles so it was slow going through the fields.

I got the job as the water boy for the crew. I was too small to reach the top of the stock of corn. Also, with the long walk down long cornrows all day long, I would not be able to keep up with the crews. My job was to have the driver take me to the water well or the farm yard to fill up four to six canvas bags of water. Sometimes the water wells were out at the end of the fields, where I could walk to get my water bags filled.

The boys and girls would be thirsty by the time they got to the other end of the field. They would also be tired and sweaty. Some of the cornrows would be half a mile long, and it would take the crews an hour or two to get through one pass of the field. The driver and I would drive around to the other end of the field, and wait for the crew to arrive.

In the morning, the crews would come out of the fields wet with dew, covered with tassel dust, mud to their knees, and cussing that they were going to quit today.

They were paid well, from eight to ten dollars an hour. They would put in twelve hours every day, six days a week. Crew chiefs received higher pay. Most of the crew chiefs had worked one or two years before becoming a crew chief. Their job was to follow the detassel crew and start pulling the tassels that the boys and girls missed on their first trip through the cornfield. Crew chiefs would supervise six people in their crew. Sometimes a crew chief would come out with his arms loaded with tassels. He would place the tassels on the ground in the row where the worker had missed all those tassels from that row. Crew chiefs would take the boy or girl to the side and give them a lecture that they had to do better than what they had done during their first trip through the row. If they continued to miss the tassels, the crew chief would tell them not to show up the next day. Some boys and girls were released from their job, midday, because they didn't pull all the tassels or they were very slow getting through the fields.

Being the water boy, I was the most popular person on the entire crew. I always had fresh water, which was cold, and a friendly smile. This was where I met a lot of older girls, such as the Tinglehoff sisters.

They were all in high school and took very good care of me. Dorothy Tinglehoff, who was the oldest of the sisters, was the head crew chief. At lunchtime, everybody took out their sack lunches or lunch boxes and climbed up underneath the shade of the semi-truck trailer. Everyone ate their lunch, and then tried to take a nap to rest their tired bodies. Everybody called Dorothy Tinglehoff by her nickname, which was Dotty. She always wanted to see what was in my lunch box. Then she would share whatever fruit or vegetable she had in her lunch box with me.

I also met the Cogan family—Mother Cogan was a crew chief, Bill, was the oldest brother, Tommy was my age, and they had a younger sister. Bill and Tommy played on the Junior Legion baseball team with Terry. They both were the jokesters of the group. They kept the spirits up for everyone on the crew, especially when they got to the end of the row of corn in the mid-afternoon hot sun, exhausted. I was to give everyone some salt tablets along with the water. Wayne, the truck driver, had the job of looking for signs of heat stroke among the crew. He drove us to the fields every day after he got his orders. He knew which fields needed to be picked from the previous night. His job lasted six to eight weeks. After the eight weeks, the crew chiefs would pick the boys and girls who were good workers.

That crew was the specialty crew with a higher rate of pay. They were the cleanup crew of the fields that the regular crews had gone through. They went through the fields to make sure there were no tassels left in the female rows. I continued to be the water boy on those expert crews. It was a lot more fun, and they didn't mind hard work.

At the end of the summer, Uncle Frank Culver from Wisconsin came to visit Papa. The two of them loaded up my clothes to take me back to the orphanage since school would start soon. Upon arriving at the home, I went downstairs to the playroom, and I found Stanley,

Sterling, and the other boys. They told me that most of the kids had moved out over the summer months, which left only twenty boys, along with fifteen girls in the orphanage. They had heard they were trying to close down the orphanage.

The superintendent sent someone down to get me to come back up to the office. When I got to the office, Papa and Uncle Frank told me to get in the car with them. I didn't even get to say goodbye to my home friends. As we drove down the long driveway to the highway, Papa turned to me in the back seat.

He said, "They have decided they will close the orphanage next month. The superintendent thought that you, Jimmy, should come and live with me."

What really happened in the superintendent's office was that the superintendent gave Papa a choice, because the state was reforming the children's orphanages throughout the state. The states were going to go to foster homes for the kids who were left over in the orphanage. Papa had to make a decision whether to put me in a foster home, put me up for adoption, or have me live with some relatives.

Papa knew that none of his children wanted me to live with them. So there again, Papa, who was already seventy-eight years old and lived alone would have to take me into his house and care for me daily, while trying to live off his retirement money.

Follow Jimmy's life and adventures in Book Two, *It Takes a Town to Raise an Orphan.*

About the Orphanage

The orphanage where Jimmy Brown grew up was started in 1889 when Rev. Axel Nordin took three children into his home. In 1907, the Evangelical Free Church became involved in finding underprivileged kids for Reverend Nordin. He now had eighty children living in his expanded home. The churches from Iowa and surrounding local areas raised money. The home board voted to build this three-story building out of brick. It was one mile west of Holdrege, Nebraska. Rev. H. A. Gustin was the first superintendent.

The construction of the building began on the flat farmland of Phillips County. The surrounding community could see this flagship orphanage from miles around. The home was called the Christian Children's Home, which housed 101 boys and girls in 1933.

When Jimmy Brown arrived in 1943, eighty boys and girls were living in the home. Ages ranged from three-year-olds to eighteen-year-old children. The Evangelical Free Church had a lot of influence upon all these children. The farmland surrounding the home had been donated or purchased by the board of trustees to provide crops to help feed the children or to provide cash crops to offset the expenses. There was a big dairy barn built three years after I came to the orphanage. The purpose was to start a triple A (AAA) milking barn. The Holstein milking herd had 100 to 125 milking cows that were milked two times daily. It supplied the milk and cash flow to offset expenses for the operations of the children's home.

Acknowledgments

The writing of this book has been an emotional endeavor into my past. I am very grateful to have had Candace Sinclair (candacesinclair.com) help guide me through these nine years of childhood experiences. Another wonderful place was the Huntington's Disease Adversary Center and a wonderful person, Kelly B. I want to thank her for her wonderful articles that explain what it really is like to have this disease, and still try to exist in this world.

I want to thank all the home kids whom I talked to during the writing of this book, in regards to the details of daily living in an orphanage that was so structured to give us a running start on life itself. Jean Meyer's conversation and her help in obtaining pictures of the orphanage brought back a lot of memories for this book.

About the Author

James Brown lives in Huntington Beach, California with his wife, Charlotte. He is a retired physical therapist who spent fifty-one years treating patients in his multiple offices and through contracts with rehab agencies for at-home patients. He and his wife have two grown sons, five grandsons, and one granddaughter. This is the first book in the three-book series about Jimmy Brown.

Don't miss out!

Visit the website below and you can sign up to receive emails whenever JAMES BROWN publishes a new book. There's no charge and no obligation.

https://books2read.com/r/B-A-QVCCB-YTESC

BOOKS 2 READ

Connecting independent readers to independent writers.

About the Author

James Brown lives in Huntington Beach, California with his wife, Charlotte. He is a retired physical therapist who spent fifty-one years treating patients in his multiple offices and through contracts with rehab agencies for at-home patients. He and his wife have two grown sons, five grandsons, and one granddaughter. This is the first book in the three-book series about Jimmy Brown, the Orphan Boy.

Read more at https://jimmybrownclub.com.